WND Books
COLLECTOR'S EDITION

THE DIVINE SECRET

The Awesome and Untold Truth
About Your Phenomenal Destiny

Joe Kovacs

**bancroft
press**

Published by Bancroft Press "Books that enlighten"
P.O. Box 65360, Baltimore, MD 21209
800-637-7377
410-764-1967 (fax)
www.bancroftpress.com

Cover & Interior design:
Tracy Copes; Daft Generation
tracy@daftgeneration.com

Hardcover / ISBN 978-1-61088-039-8 / $22.99
Paperback / ISBN 978-1-61088-040-4 / $14.95
Printed in the United States of America
First Edition
1 3 5 7 9 10 8 6 4 2

To all the members of "the whole family in heaven and earth." (Ephesians 3:15)

This includes our eternal Father and His Son, Jesus, as well as their children who have been imbued with the Holy Spirit or have witnessed and responded to its power. You probably know many of their names. Some of God's more famous champions include Noah, Enoch, Abraham, Sarah, Jacob, Joseph, Moses, Joshua, Samuel, Samson, Gideon, David, Elijah, Elisha, Daniel, Shadrach, Meshach, Abednego, Isaiah, Jeremiah, Hosea, Jonah, Micah, Zechariah, Mary, Matthew, Mark, Luke, John, Peter, Paul, James, and Jude. These are ordinary, real people who lived extraordinary lives, and we'll see every one of them with our own eyes.

It also includes the countless other children of God whose names may or may not be recorded in the pages of Scripture, but who, during the vast epochs of time, decided to serve the Most High God and seek immortal life in Their glorious kingdom. I hope this includes you.

Table of Contents

Introduction 1
Chapter 1: Do You Want to Know A Secret? 9
    It's No Secret 14
    In the Real Beginning 17
    The Family in Heaven 23
    In Our Image and Our Likeness 26
    Would You Be So Kind? 27
    Man of the Hour 30
    The Children of God 32
    That's Just Divine 40

Chapter 2: The Quickening 49
    The Ingredients 53
    Born of the Spirit 56
    The Changing 61
    Second Coming Attraction 69
    Shine Like the Son 76
    Divine Dining 82
    Knowledge Is Power 89
    Now You See Me, Now You Don't 91
    Matter of Fact 95
Chapter 3: The Kingdom of God 103
    Paradise Found 110
    The Government 124
    Life Does Have Meaning 140
    Good News! There's Hope for Others 153
    The Rest of the Dead 156
    Here Comes the Judgment 161
    Amazing Patience 171
Subject Index
Scripture Index

Introduction

Hi. My name is Joe. I'm no great thing and I won't pretend to be. I'm just an ordinary guy, a news reporter by trade, and I have a secret I wish to share with you. It revolves around some amazing news—probably the best news you've ever heard—and it deals with your personal future. Yes, I'm talking to you, the person holding this book in your hands right this second.

I have no doubts about what's coming for you. At least, I know what's intended for you, and it's something wonderful beyond compare, and it's something you can make a reality. I want you to know and understand this secret because once you do, the rest of your life will have so much more meaning than you ever thought possible. At this very moment, stunning information about your personal destiny is readily available to you. In fact, the information has been available for quite some time, but too few people are really looking with their eyes and minds wide open to the truth.

This information is probably not listed in your Facebook profile or stored somewhere in your iPhone. It's definitely not in your school files or in your birth records. But you can access it right now, because I'm going to tell you all about it in considerable detail in the coming pages.

How can I know, with such certainty, what's meant for you? I do something surprisingly simple. I open up the Bible, read the words on its pages, and actually believe them. I know that may sound strange in a day and age when so many people think it's uncool to read ancient Scripture from a book that claims to be the source of truth.

Well, if it makes you happy, you can think I'm bonkers. It doesn't bother me. But you really should want to know the truth about your life and your intended destiny because it's most likely *not* what you've been led to believe, even if you're a devout Christian who has spent years going to church. You're not going to dwell on a cloud with a harp in your hands, doing a whole bunch of nothingness for all eternity.

If you're wondering whether I'm a Christian . . . the answer is absolutely yes! I wholeheartedly worship Jesus Christ of Nazareth as God, and believe that none of us is saved without Him. I also think the Bible is the inspired Word of God, and it's our instruction manual for living. I just wish more people would read it. If they did, there'd likely be much less of a need for books like this one explaining to everyone what they can find out for themselves.

This is actually my second book. My first one is called *Shocked by the Bible: The Most Astonishing Facts You've Never Been Told.* That was basically a giant news report about what's included in Scripture, and what's not. When it instantly rocketed to #1 on Amazon.com upon its publication in 2008, I myself was shocked. I had written it to clear up people's misconceptions about Scripture, and to encourage folks to crack open the Bible to read it for themselves and see what's really there as well as what's not there.

For some reason, that book made plenty of people angry. Who'da thunk that prompting people to read their own Bibles would be so controversial? Some people actually called up radio stations, urging management not to allow me on the air to talk about the book. They may have been under the mistaken impression I was somehow trashing the Bible or attacking Christianity—there was no truth to either. As I said, I'm a Bible believer just hoping that people read and accept what's in their own Bibles. So to all those mean-spirited buttinskis out there, I humbly request that you please get a life.

I began writing about Scripture only because I was fed up with hearing so many mistakes and untruths in public discourse about the Bible's content. Whether it comes from television news, radio talk shows, or even church leaders and those who attend services, there's an extraordinary amount of biblical illiteracy these days. It's really quite sad.

Even today, despite my best efforts with *Shocked by the Bible*, there remain some very common misconceptions on the most basic of facts. Many people still think that three wise men came to visit Jesus in a manger the night He was born in Bethlehem. It's simply false. The truth is that no wise men at all saw Jesus lying in a manger. Only shepherds were in attendance that night. Yes, it is true that *some* wise men (the Bible never specifies how many) did eventually show up later, when Jesus was a *young child* in a *house*, not a babe in a manger. How do we know? Because of the words on the page. The New Testament actually says wise men met Jesus for the first time when the boy was a young child in a house. It's as simple as that, folks.

Also, there were not just two of each kind of animal aboard Noah's ark. There were actually seven pairs of the clean animals—those fit for eating—and only two each of the animals not meant for eating. Did the ark land on Mount Ararat? If you think yes, please crack open your own Bible and read Genesis 8:4, which tells you something different. It says the ark rested upon the *mountains of Ararat*. Though it's only a single letter "s" tacked onto the word *mountain*, I think we can all agree there's a big difference between *Mount Ararat* and the *mountains of Ararat*.

If you haven't yet read *Shocked by the Bible*, I urge you to do so, even if it's after this book, because you'll get a lifetime's worth of accurate Bible knowledge in just a few hours of reading.

But back to the future. The Bible means what it says and says what it means, and when you embrace the words that are already printed, you'll learn a divine secret about your life now and in the years ahead. Ironically, it's not really a secret at all for those who bother to look into it. It's perhaps the most obvious secret ever that's been hiding in plain sight for centuries. There's something breathtakingly awesome coming your way, something that provides much-needed hope and understanding for all of us in these turbulent times. It's what your Creator has had in mind for you since long before you were born—since long before *anyone* in the history of mankind was born.

I suspect you've got some big questions about the most important issues of life, and chances are, you've never received a satisfactory answer to them. The questions might include "Why are we all here?," "What's the meaning of life?," "What is God actually doing with people?," "What will we be doing once Jesus returns?" and "What about people who never heard the message of God or don't believe now? Are they forever done for?" Even people who attend church services for decades may never hear these deep and critical issues thoroughly addressed. Or if the questions are brought up, people might hear some wimpy response such as, "Oh, some things are just not meant for us to know," or "I guess we'll find out after we're dead."

After we're dead? You gotta be kiddin' me!

In the 1980s, a rock band called Missing Persons had a big hit with its song, "Destination Unknown." The song's basic message is that life is so strange when you don't know your destination. While that's completely true, there's simply no need to be in the dark. There's no reason to live your life in a zombie-like state, either ignorant or brain-dead when it comes to your true, intended destination. You *can* understand the most important issues and what's always been meant for you. There *are* clear, solid answers, and they're vividly spelled out in the Bible. Your destination *is* known, and it's most likely not what you've been told.

Perhaps many people remain in a state of confusion only because they just don't read the Bible regularly. Don't be embarrassed if that's you, because the vast majority of people in the world are in that club. Others may casually read Scripture now and then, but they fail to grasp the glorious truth being shouted at them. Even the most devoted fans of God's Word might think the Bible cannot possibly mean what it says when it comes to what God has designed for everyone, because the answers may seem too good to be true. It's quite common for someone to think, "I'm not worthy!"

In this book, I'm going to call your attention to many actual, underpublicized quotes from your own Bible that will finally shine some light on the situation and answer many of the deepest questions about life and what lies ahead. To put the greatest possible emphasis on them, I'm putting *every personal remark by God in red letters*, from both the *Old Testament* and the New Testament. I have no idea why Bible publishers generally have red-letter editions of the New Testament alone, as if the God of the Old Testament is somehow different from that of the New. God is eternal, and I think *all* of His direct comments need to be highlighted in *every* instance of Scripture.

There's a brilliant, divinely ordained plan in the works that's so fantastic and so wondrous, it may at first be too difficult for your mind to completely absorb and handle. Nevertheless, it's true, and you can finally see the message with your own eyes. When you read the Bible as you would any other book, without any blinders of man-made tradition or the influence of pagan religions, this great mystery becomes as clear as day.

But beware. I suspect some people, especially those who rely on tradition more than anything else, may try to convince you the Bible doesn't mean what it says when it comes to the real reason you're alive, your intended purpose, and your spectacular future. Thankfully, they can't erase the words of Scripture that proclaim it.

As I always say, I'm not here to force you to believe anything in particular. You're completely free to choose what to believe and which path to follow. My role is merely to show you the Bible words that not only unveil the secret, but also reveal what it means. You see, the Good Book explains itself when all the puzzle pieces are neatly arranged. And please don't take my word for something just because I say or write it. The Bible says to "prove all things" (1 Thessalonians 5:21 KJV), so feel free to look it all up for yourself. I want people following God and His word, and certainly not me.

An awakening is taking place now all across the planet. People are being aroused from their slumber on a plethora of issues, whether they're political or spiritual ones. Will you be among those who continue to snooze away in dreamland, or are you ready to wake up to the mind-boggling truth—the divine secret of your phenomenal future?

Chapter 1

Do You Want to Know A Secret?

Is there something really important about your future that you're not being told?

Is there some crucial information that discloses your intended destiny, but for whatever reason has not found its way into your head?

Is there an epic secret that's been kept under wraps for virtually the entirety of human existence—a mystery so magnificent you just might have trouble believing it once you unlock it?

Even if you were fully aware of such a hidden treasure of information, what would you do with it? Would you be willing to make changes in your life to turn the secret into reality? Or would you just leave it alone and continue with your routine, day-to-day existence?

Well, have I got news for you! The secret you're about to find out is big news—tremendously good news, and probably the best news you could ever imagine for you personally.

It's not a traditional secret in the sense of being an entry in someone's diary. It's not someone's hidden romantic desire—a secret yearning to love someone else. It's not a state secret, packed with intrigue, obtained when governments engage in dangerous, unseemly, covert action. It's not a secret diplomatic cable that's been leaked on the Internet. And it's not some kind of a trade secret, such as the formula for Coca-Cola or the Colonel's "secret recipe" of herbs and spices for Kentucky Fried Chicken.

It's a secret of infinite proportions, and one that would change the course of human history if it were common knowledge. In fact, had this secret been generally known two thousand years ago, the man named Jesus of Nazareth, according to your very own Bible, would not have been crucified. And if the entire world knew it today and put it into action, people wouldn't be fretting about Armageddon, because the so-called "end of the world" would never arrive. While the world as a whole will neither learn nor accept the secret in this lifetime, we as individuals can do so, and embrace its magnificent blessings.

It's high time you learn what this secret is, and understand the true meaning of not only your life and ultimate destiny, but also the lives and destinies of countless others.

The word "secret" itself is a fascinating, enthralling term. It's an expression that tends to stop people in their tracks, prompting them to pay attention. Dictionaries define it as a mystery—as something hidden or unexplained, along with something kept from the knowledge of others or shared only confidentially with a few.

Everyone has secrets, whether they be good ones, bad ones, or ones that nobody gives a flying hoot about. Some people go to extraordinary lengths to hold onto their secrets, while others have less of a problem sharing them. But virtually everyone seems to be engrossed by knowledge and information, especially when he or she thinks it's been concealed.

Now add the word "divine" to the word "secret," and you heighten interest in finding out what's been hidden. Since millions of people seek a connection to the divine, unseen world of God, there has to be something really special and juicy about a "divine secret," doesn't there? Just what might that divine secret be? Is there some sort of God-inspired mystery that hasn't been unsealed, or some special information that's gone untrumpeted for thousands of years? If so, what is it? And where can it be located?

The answers can actually be found in the Holy Bible, the ultimate source of written truth. Though it's the bestselling book of all time, it's also among the least understood. You probably already know that the Bible is a book about many things, including inspiration, history, sex, prophecy (which is actually news events written before they happen), revelations about the Creator of all things, and instructions for mankind on the proper way to live. But it's also about something else.

In case you've never thought of it this way, the Bible is actually a book containing a truly divine secret. It's not a fictional mystery you might see in a novel, children's storybook tale, or Hollywood movie. It's not a guessing game of some kind or a mathematical secret buried in numeric codes written in ancient languages. The Bible itself outright declares it contains a divine secret—in fact, more than one secret, all of which are fascinating mysteries about God and human beings.

Some passages in assorted Bible translations refer to "God's secret," "God's secret wisdom," "God's mysterious plan," "a wonderful secret," "the secret that was hidden from everyone," "the secret of the Good News," "the mysteries of God," and "the mysteries of the kingdom of God."

Wow! Scripture makes it more than obvious that God has a mysterious, secret plan, so let's take a look at some of the quotations that mention it. Perhaps the single most declarative verse about the Bible's divine secret is found in the New Testament, in the book of Colossians, stating:

> This message is the secret that was hidden from everyone since the beginning of time ... (Colossians 1:26 NCV)

There it is, right on the page of your own Bible. The apostle Paul talked about some sort of secret hidden from everyone since the human clock started ticking. Please feel free to check your favorite version of Scripture, and you'll discover it discusses a secret or mystery that's been kept under wraps throughout the ages.

But if you think this is just some rogue sentence that's either a mistranslation or simply doesn't belong in the Bible, please think again. Paul used very similar language numerous times elsewhere, as he discussed:

> ... the mystery kept secret since the world began ... (Romans 16:25 NKJV)

> But we speak the wisdom of God in a mystery, the hidden wisdom which God ordained before the ages ... (1 Corinthians 2:7 NKJV)

Once again, Paul cited a certain plan of God, labeling it a mystery kept secret from the beginning. These are not my words. They're the words of the Holy Bible, and I encourage you to crack open your own Bible and read them yourself. As Paul continued his thought in 1 Corinthians, he admitted that Jesus would never have been executed if the people in charge at that time comprehended this mysterious plan: "None of the rulers of this world understood it. If they had, they would not have crucified the Lord of glory." (1 Corinthians 2:8 NCV)

Paul also taught that those who follow the truth are actually special agents of sorts: "So then, men ought to regard us as servants of Christ and as those entrusted with the secret things of God." (1 Corinthians 4:1 NIV)

Did you catch what Paul said? People who are servants of Christ are actually entrusted with the secret things of God. There are indeed some things hidden from the world's general population, but true followers of Jesus are meant to know the secret things.

But Paul wasn't alone in addressing this. Jesus Christ, God Himself in the flesh, used terms including "secret" and "mysteries." In fact, when Jesus was asked directly about why He so often spoke to people in puzzling analogies known as parables instead of just explaining things simply and clearly, He gave an answer that even today surprises many Christians who wrongly assume Jesus was the great communicator-in-chief. Jesus indicated He was purposely HIDING His message from the vast majority of the public, intending it only for a select few at that time. Here's what He told His apostles:

> You are permitted to understand the secret about the Kingdom of God. But I am using these stories to conceal everything about it from outsiders. (Mark 4:11 NLT)

> To you it has been given to know the mysteries of the kingdom of God, but to the rest it is given in parables, that 'Seeing they may not see, And hearing they may not understand.' (Luke 8:10 NKJV)

> Because it has been given to you to know the mysteries of the kingdom of heaven, but to them it has not been given. (Matthew 13:11 NKJV)

> Jesus used stories to tell all these things to the people; he always used stories to teach them. This

is as the prophet said: "I will speak using stories; I will tell things that have been secret since the world was made." (Matthew 13:34-35 NCV)

Yes, you're reading those quotes correctly. If you've been under the impression that Jesus was sent to Earth to clear things up and make everything easy to understand in an instant, you're no doubt stunned. That notion is simply untrue, according to Scripture. Jesus more than once said some things had been kept secret since the world was made. He stressed that He was taking deliberate steps to conceal the secrets, to hide the mysteries of God's kingdom from the general populace, yet at the same time was revealing the divine secret only to His closest followers.

It's No Secret

The situation is drenched with irony, because while the Bible goes out of its way to let us know a divine secret exists, it also mentions that people are glorified when they try to discover what God has hidden: "It is the glory of God to conceal a matter; to search out a matter is the glory of kings." (Proverbs 25:2 NIV)

Moreover, Scripture indicates that God at times unwraps secrets, at least for certain people. For instance, in the Old Testament, we read of God's prophet Daniel and a Babylonian king named Nebuchadnezzar, both of whom acknowledged that God is the one who reveals secret information. Referring to God, Daniel said, "He gives wisdom to the wise And knowledge to those who have understanding. He reveals deep and secret things . . ." (Daniel 2:21-22 NKJV)

As Daniel was helping the king understand a disturbing dream, Daniel again noted: "But there is a God in heaven who reveals secrets . . ." (Daniel 2:28 NKJV)

And after Daniel had informed Nebuchadnezzar of the dream's content and its proper interpretation forecasting future events, even the pagan monarch declared, "Truly your God is the God of gods, the Lord of kings, and a revealer of secrets . . ." (Daniel 2:47 NKJV)

Elsewhere in the Old Testament, we find statements indicating that God's hidden information will be made known:

> The secret of the LORD is with those who fear Him, And He will show them His covenant. (Psalm 25:14 NKJV)

> Surely the Lord GOD does nothing, Unless He reveals His secret to His servants the prophets. (Amos 3:7 NKJV)

I don't wish to sound like a broken record, but it's amazing how often the Bible clearly says secret, hidden information exists, *and* that it does become disclosed. The New Testament agrees, and has a variety of examples confirming this. The gospel of Matthew states:

> At that time Jesus said, "I praise you, Father, Lord of heaven and earth, because you have HIDDEN these things from the wise and learned, and REVEALED them to little children." (Matthew 11:25 NIV, emphasis added)

> And in the gospel of Luke, Jesus noted, "For nothing is secret that will not be revealed, nor anything hidden that will not be known and come to light." (Luke 8:17 NKJV)

That's right, secrets will be revealed, and what's surprising to many folks is that we don't have to wait until we die or until Jesus comes back to find out one of the best secrets—the divine secret that involves you and your future.

In the book of Ephesians, Paul indicated he was personally selected by God to reveal what had been concealed: "I was chosen to explain to everyone this plan that God, the Creator of all things, had kept secret from the beginning." (Ephesians 3:9 NLT)

A few chapters later, he made this request of his fellow Christians: "Also pray for me that when I speak, God will give me words so that I can tell the secret of the Good News without fear." (Ephesians 6:19 NCV)

Once again, Scripture plainly talks about "the secret of the Good News," and once again it mentions that a servant of God—in this case, Paul—was looking to announce that secret fearlessly back in his own day! Yes, back in the days when the New Testament was being compiled. It's not meant to be a secret that's kept from you or me or anyone for the past two millennia. In other words, it's no secret! At least, it's no secret any longer, and anyone and everyone can know it. It's meant to be revealed. It's meant to be trumpeted. It's meant to be proclaimed throughout the land. And it's meant to be understood by the servants of God:

> This message is the secret that was hidden from everyone since the beginning of time, but now it is made known to God's holy people. (Colossians 1:26 NCV)

That's the verse I opened this chapter with, but now I've provided the entire sentence to stress that it's not a mystery anymore. It's now made known to those following God, to those who want to learn.

Are you finally curious? Do you want to learn what this exclusive, long-hidden knowledge actually is? Are you daring enough to take off the blinders and dump all those preconceived notions and assumptions that may have held you back from understanding the actual Good News, which is what the word "gospel" literally means? Do you genuinely wish to find out what's truly meant for your life, the lives of your family and friends, and the real reason why we're all here? Are you willing to let the Bible speak for itself and accept the words actually written on its pages, even when some people will tell you the Bible doesn't really mean what it says? And once you learn the sensational secret, are you going to embrace it, cherish it, and share it with others, or will you be among those who ignore it or continue to hide it?

There's nothing to fear. The time has come for the incredible truth of your intended destiny to be unveiled, understood, and broadcast. It's time to reveal the divine secret.

In the Real Beginning

To understand what the divine secret is and the fantastic future it holds for you, let's start by traveling back in time. After all, we've read that the message is "the secret that was hidden from everyone since the beginning of time," as well as a "mystery, the hidden wisdom which God ordained before the ages."

So let's journey back. Way back. Back before television shows transitioned from black-and-white to color, back before atomic weaponry was developed. Let's travel to a period when there were no such things as cities and countries. Back before the very first line of the Bible, which says, "In the beginning God created the heavens and the earth." (Genesis 1:1 NKJV)

Let's go back to a period before there were planets, and back before the stars were created. We're traveling far back into cosmic antiquity to the beginning. I mean the real beginning. The Bible itself actually reveals a time prior to the creation of everything material you currently see and feel around you. This super-ancient epoch is found in the first chapter of the gospel of John, where we read the famous opening lines, "In the beginning was the Word, and the Word was with God, and the Word was God.

He was in the beginning with God." (John 1:1-2 NKJV)

It's here in the deepest recesses of the cosmic past, before the creation of the physical universe, where we're introduced to two beings—the Word and God—both of whom happen to be God.

But who is the Word? And who is God? And how can both of these figures be called "God?"

To answer these questions, it's important to understand some key information.

First of all, God is described throughout countless translations of the Bible as being "spirit." The King James Version, for instance, declares: "God is a Spirit." (John 4:24) Many other translations leave out the indefinite article, and just simply state that "God is Spirit."

Either way, it means that God is not composed of the physical, fleshy material from the ground that make up the ingredients inside you and me. God doesn't consist of any element on the periodic table, such as hydrogen, oxygen, helium, or gold. God is not a carbon-based being. (I guess that means God doesn't have a carbon footprint either. But I digress.)

God is comprised of something other than matter. That something else is called spirit. The Bible itself notes that "a spirit does not have flesh and bones" (Luke 24:39 NKJV). So God is actually composed of spirit, not being made up of flesh or physical matter as we know it.

The second important point is that the English word "God" is translated from a Hebrew word that is not singular, but plural. That's correct—PLURAL, as in more than one. The original term that's translated as "God" in the book of Genesis in your very own Bible is *Elohim*, a plural word in Hebrew.

You may never have heard or understood that before, but it's completely consistent with what we've read so far dating back to the real beginning, with more than one person mentioned. Remember, the Bible indicates "the Word was with God, and the Word was God. He was in the beginning with God." (John 1:1-2 NKJV)

If you're having trouble comprehending this, here's a brief analogy to make the concept a bit easier to understand. Take a look at these two sentences:

> In the room, there was Nancy, and Nancy was with Reagan, and Nancy was Reagan. She was in the room with Reagan.

Here, you probably can grasp the notion that there were two different people in a room together, both of whom happen to be Reagan. Nancy, whose last name is Reagan, was one person in the room, and someone else named Reagan, such as her presidential husband Ronald, was also there, but he's being referred to only by his last name, the Reagan family name. Thus, Nancy can be with Reagan, and also be Reagan at the same time. In the same way, the Word can be with God, as well as be God simultaneously. They are two different persons—two separate individuals who share a common, singular name.

In the English language today, there are many words that sound singular but actually have a plural connotation. The word "team" is like that. If I were to tell you that the basketball team is flying across country for its next game, your mind immediately recognizes that this one team mentioned actually refers to a bunch of people making the trip.

The word "company" is another example, so if I said the entire car company is getting a huge bonus this year, you'd realize that more than one person could expect a bigger paycheck. The word "family" is a classic case of a word sounding singular but having a plural meaning. If I said the Osmond family is going to hold a reunion in the Caribbean, then you'd expect more than one person and scores of dazzling teeth to be making travel arrangements. And if I were to mention the entire human family, this singular concept would, in the vocal style of astronomer Carl Sagan, bring to mind "billions and billions" of people.

So, the question remains: Who exactly is "the Word"?

I'll make this as clear as I can for you. "The Word" refers to the spirit-composed God being who actually did the creating. During that super-ancient time period before the world was formed, this creating agent was known as "the Word."

The first chapter of John, which again is the real start of the Bible, makes it obvious that the Word is the one doing the work of creation: "All things were made through Him, and without Him nothing was made that was made." (John 1:3 NKJV)

Much later in time, this Creator God, "the Word," left His place in the unseen spirit dimension of heaven to live life as a regular, physical human being, and went by the name of Jesus Christ of Nazareth. How do we know? Because this very same first chapter of John goes on to make the connection.

Verse 10 says, "He was in the world, and the world was made through Him, and the world did not know Him." Verse 14 states it plainly: **"And the Word became flesh and dwelt among us, and we beheld His glory, the glory as of the only begotten of the Father."** (emphasis added)

Yes, this eternal spirit being who made our planet and everything else actually became a flesh-and-blood human being and lived here as an ordinary person. He has been alive forever, never having been created by someone else and never having had a birthday in the unseen, spirit dimension prior to His arrival in a Bethlehem manger. The Old Testament prophet Micah spoke of His eternal origins, explaining His "goings forth have been from of old, from everlasting." (Micah 5:2 KJV)

So it was Jesus, all the way back to the time before creation, who was simply known as "the Word." John also refers to Jesus as "the Word of life" (1 John 1:1 KJV), and the last book of the Bible confirms the Word name for Jesus, explaining that "His name is called The Word of God." (Revelation 19:13 NKJV)

Incidentally, it's not just John who identified Jesus as the Creator of all things. The idea is echoed elsewhere in Scripture, including the book of Colossians, which, referring to Jesus, says: "For by Him all things were created that are in heaven and that are on earth, visible and invisible, whether thrones or dominions or principalities or powers. All things were created through Him and for Him." (1:16 NKJV)

And recall what Paul said about the divine secret, calling it "the mystery, which from the beginning of the ages has been hidden in God who created all things through Jesus Christ." (Ephesians 3:9 NKJV)

The Bible means what it says. Everything that was made—whether it's the ground we walk on, the gold and silver buried in the hills, the massive variety of plants, the wide array of animals (both the majestic-looking ones as well as the funny-faced ones), the air we breathe, the foods we eat, the water we drink and swim in, human beings themselves, or positions of power both here on Earth and in the unseen realm of heaven—was made personally by Jesus Christ and for Jesus Christ.

Thus, Jesus, who was known as "the Word" far back in the deepest reaches of time, is the one who handled the formation of everything. In Isaiah we read:

> This is what the LORD says—your Redeemer, who formed you in the womb: I am the LORD, who has made all things, who alone stretched out the heavens, who spread out the earth by myself. (44:24 NIV)

Understanding the concept of Jesus as the Creator is the very first key to unlocking the divine secret, and will help decipher the rest of the mystery of why we're all here, what we're meant to become in the future, and what we're intended to be doing.

Now, as we've read, Jesus was not alone back in the real beginning. During the time He was known as "the Word," Jesus existed with someone else. This someone else is initially called "God" in the very first verses of John's gospel, but later in John and in other books of the Bible, He is referred to as "Father."

Many times in the New Testament, you'll find phrases such as "God the Father" or "God our Father," and they're often in a sentence that also mentions Jesus, and makes a distinction between God the Father and Jesus.

For instance, Paul stated:

> I was made an apostle through Jesus Christ and God the Father who raised Jesus from the dead. (Galatians 1:1 NCV)

John declared:

> Grace, mercy, and peace will be with you from God the Father and from the Lord Jesus Christ, the Son of the Father ... (2 John 1:3 NKJV)

> He who abides in the doctrine of Christ has both the Father and the Son. (2 John 1:9 NKJV)

And the author of Hebrews said:

But God said this about his Son: "God, your throne will last forever and ever. You will rule your kingdom with fairness." (Hebrews 1:8 NCV)

Note here that God the Father clearly called His Son Jesus by the name "God" as well!

During the thirty-three years that He walked on Earth, Jesus, whose name in Hebrew is Yeshua, actually spoke about some of His ancient, pre-creation existence with His Father. He specifically mentioned it during His final prayer shortly before being put to death.

As He addressed His Father in heaven, Jesus said, "you loved me before the world was made." (John 17:24 NCV)

Jesus also implored His Father to return Him to the glorious state the two had shared even before Planet Earth was brought into existence: "And now, Father, give me glory with you; give me the glory I had with you before the world was made." (John 17:5 NCV)

It's unmistakable. Jesus shared a glorious state with God the Father before the creation of the world was ever commenced. These are some of the most stunning and profound verses of the entire Bible, and they certainly don't get enough attention, even in many Christian circles today. They're immensely important because they help reveal more about the mysterious divine secret.

The Family in Heaven

Knowing what we know so far, that both Jesus Christ (also known as the Word) and God the Father are both spirit-composed beings who have been related to each other for eons dating back to long before the universe was created, helps us realize exactly what God actually is—and that, my friends, is a family.

Yes, God is indeed a family. Jesus is the Word and He's one member of the God family, and God the Father is yet another member of that same God family. It may sound somewhat strange to your ears to hear about the God family, but the Bible itself, using that exact phrase, states that God is a family in heaven.

Paul declared, "For this reason I bow my knees to the Father of our Lord Jesus Christ, from whom the whole family in heaven and earth is named." (Ephesians 3:14-15 NKJV)

Scripture openly declares that there's a "family in heaven," and it's named for the Father of our Lord Jesus Christ. And to state what should be obvious, the term "father" itself is a family term. Countless times throughout all Bibles, you see names referring to God the Father and Jesus the Son, members of the same family. Here's a quick sampling:

> The Father loves the Son, and has given all things into His hand. (John 3:35 NKJV)

> No one has seen God at any time. The only begotten Son, who is in the bosom of the Father, He has declared Him. (John 1:18 NKJV)

> In fact, the Father judges no one, but he has given the Son power to do all the judging. (John 5:22 NCV)

> Jesus answered and said to him, "If anyone loves Me, he will keep My word; and My Father will love him, and We will come to him and make Our home with him." (John 14:23 NKJV)

These verses not only demonstrate the family terms of father and son, but they once again confirm the plural nature of the God family, which is made up of different persons. As we've just read, Jesus said WE (referring to Himself and the Father) will come to anyone who believes, and make OUR home with that believer. He uses plural pronouns of *we* and *our*, not *I* and *my*. Scripture also states that God the Father judges no one. But we're told another member of the God family, known as the Son, is the one given power to do all the judging. The point is, there's more than one person in this single family called God.

If we take another look at Jesus' final prayer before His execution, it's more than apparent He was not praying to Himself. He was praying to that other member of the God family known as the Father. He told his Father who was dwelling in the unseen spirit dimension of heaven: "I have glorified You on the earth. I have finished the work which You have given Me to do." (John 17:4 NKJV)

These are obviously not the same person. Jesus said He was given work to do by someone else, specifically His Father, and the work was completed.

And just as in your own family, it's even possible for these members of the God family to have a different will on a certain matter. We're shown this when Jesus asked His Father if He could possibly get out of His own pending torture and execution:

> He knelt down and prayed, saying, "Father, if it is Your will, take this cup away from Me; nevertheless not My will, but Yours, be done." (Luke 22:41-42 NKJV)

The New Century Version puts it this way:

> "Father, if you are willing, take away this cup of suffering. But do what you want, not what I want."

It's astonishing, yet ever so revealing about the nature of God's family. The desire of Jesus was actually different from the will of His Father, even though Jesus acknowledged that He'd accept the will of His Father. Of course, He eventually did accept it, and went through a horrific whipping and crucifixion.

In Our Image and Our Likeness

All right, now that you have some background, here's where things really begin to get interesting. This one God family, which is made up of more than one person, decided long ago that They (yes, They) were going to have children. Apparently, those in the God family wanted kids. Their own sons. Their own daughters. Their own offspring. All this can be found in your own Bible, and you're going to be told exactly where, so listen up.

When the Bible first speaks of the creation of human beings, God did not say "Let Me make man in My image, after My likeness." You're simply not going to find that statement in any Bible. Good luck in locating it, because it's just not there.

What you will find when you read carefully is that "God said, 'Let US make man in OUR image, according to OUR likeness.'" (Genesis 1:26, NKJV, emphasis added). This should not be a surprise, because, as we've seen, the original word for God— *Elohim* in Hebrew—is a plural term.

Here is this all-important verse in a variety of translations so you can see how consistent the versions are in revealing the plural nature of the God family:

> And God said, "Let us make man in our image, after our likeness." (KJV)

> Then God said, "Let us make human beings in our image and likeness." (NCV)

> Then God said, "Let us make man in our image, in our likeness." (NIV)

> Then God said, "Let us make human beings in our image, to be like us." (NLT)

Is it beginning to sink in yet? The Bible declares that the God family includes more than one person, referring to those in the family as *us*, and They said They were making man in Their own image, according to Their own likeness.

Would You Be So Kind?

As to the sequence of when all this took place, the creation of man came immediately after the creation of plant and animal life. It's important to note that everything was initially manufactured according to its own kind, as the Bible puts it:

> Then God said, "Let the earth bring forth grass, the herb that yields seed, and the fruit tree that yields fruit according to its kind, whose seed is in itself, on the earth"; and it was so. And the earth brought forth grass, the herb that yields seed according to its kind, and the tree that yields fruit, whose seed is in itself according to its kind. (Genesis 1:11-12, NKJV)

> So God created great sea creatures and every living thing that moves, with which the waters abounded, according to their kind, and every winged bird according to its kind. (Genesis 1:21, NKJV)

> Then God said, "Let the earth bring forth the living creature according to its kind: cattle and creeping thing and beast of the earth, each according to its kind"; and it was so. And God made the beast of the earth according to its kind, cattle according to its kind, and everything that creeps on the earth according to its kind. (Genesis 1:24-25, NKJV)

Notice how all these life forms on Earth were made after their own kind, a kind that existed either in reality in the unseen dimension of heaven or in a planned pattern there. Either way, once all of the plants, trees, birds, fish, elephants, hippos, dogs, and cats were created after their own kind, God began a whole new category of creation.

Suddenly, the God family then said, "Let Us make man in Our image, according to Our likeness." Man was being made not after a plant kind or an animal kind, but after the God kind. Together, God the Father and Jesus Christ made the decision to create man after Their very own kind, after Their own image, after Their own likeness, designed to look like members of the God family, or as the New Living Translation phrases it, "to be like us."

Can you sense more of the divine secret bubbling up to the surface yet?

God—that is to say, the divine God family—decided to begin the process of reproduction, creating human beings after Their own kind, in the image and likeness of Their own family. In fact, the Bible refers to the very first man created, named Adam, as "the son of God" (Luke 3:38 NKJV), since he had no human father, but was generated out of the ground by Jesus Himself.

For those who have never read about the creation of the first human person, it's found in Genesis 2:7: "Then the Lord God took dust from the ground and formed a man from it. He breathed the breath of life into the man's nose, and the man became a living person." (NCV)

If we could have been there to watch this fascinating scene unfold, or if it were accurately portrayed in a movie—Hollywood has a bad habit of getting Bible stories wrong—we'd see Jesus, a spirit being before He was born as a human, appearing in the same general form as a man, because man was made in the image and likeness of God. We'd see Him in his role as Creator, perhaps getting down on His hands and knees, scooping together a big wad of dust, dirt, and/or clay to begin the work. (Incidentally, if you're among the millions brainwashed into thinking human life originated in the sea, you've been lied to. People actually came from the dirt, not the water!) Once Jesus gathered enough earth, He then shaped it into the general form of—are you ready for this?—Himself! Finally, He breathed right into the man's dirt-composed nose (some translations use the word "nostrils"), and suddenly this non-living mound of dirt sculpted into the shape of God was transformed into the first living human being, a guy named Adam.

As I pointed out in *Shocked by the Bible*, members of the God family resemble you and me when it comes to shape and form. Indeed, they are always depicted as having the bodily characteristics of humans. It's actually the other way around: Humans resemble those in the God family because the Father and Jesus existed before humans. But the Bible reveals they each have a head, hair, face, eyes, nose, mouth, lips, arms, hands, fingers, torso, waist, legs, feet, and an audible voice. God is not some ethereal cloud or some bodiless energy source floating throughout the visible, as well as unseen, universe. And please forgive me if this sounds irreverent, because it's not meant to be at all, but there's never any mention of beaks, tails, paws, hooves, fins, or scales when it comes to the looks of God and man. Those attributes are found only among animals and some angels.

God's body, though comprised of spirit instead of flesh and blood, indeed looks like ours. I won't go through the whole list of verses I provided in *Shocked by the Bible*, but just a few of the highlights reveal some of God's physical attributes, with emphasis added to underscore the characteristics of the creating family:

> His HEAD and HAIR were white like wool, as white as snow, and His EYES like a flame of fire. His FEET were like fine brass, as if refined in a furnace, and His VOICE as the sound of many waters ... (Revelation 1:14-15 NKJV)

> I made the earth and all the people living on it. With MY OWN HANDS I stretched out the skies ... (Isaiah 45:12 NCV)

> And when He had made an end of speaking with him on Mount Sinai, He gave Moses two tablets of the Testimony, tablets of stone, written with the FINGER of God. (Exodus 31:18 NKJV)

> The glory of the LORD shall be revealed, And all flesh shall see it together; For the MOUTH of the LORD has spoken. (Isaiah 40:5 NKJV)

Yes, God has body parts, and they look like yours. He even sits down and stands up like you and I do, and is described in both those bodily positions. Colossians 3:1 tells us "where Christ is, sitting at the right hand of God." (NKJV)

And Acts 7:55 indicates: "But Stephen, full of the Holy Spirit, gazed steadily into heaven and saw the glory of God, and he saw Jesus standing in the place of honor at God's right hand." (NLT)

It should be absolutely clear that human beings have been designed in the same general form and shape as their Maker.

Man of the Hour

Now that the creation of the first man, Adam, is on the record, you might be wondering to yourself, "Just what is man, anyway?" Or perhaps it crosses your mind as, "What's the deal? Why did this creation take place?"

Don't worry, you're not alone with such questions, because everyone really wants to know the reasons behind the plan. The incredible answers, which you're about to see with your own eyes from your very own Bible, will help unlock and explain a major portion of the divine secret.

We already know that man was created in the image and likeness of God. But why is that? What's the real significance? There had to be a special reason for the God family to say, "Let Us make man in Our image, according to Our likeness," when everything else, from apples to zebras, was created after its own respective kind.

The staggering answer goes along with what we've already seen in Scripture. It's something that can be summed up in this simple sentence: The God family is actually having many children, and when Jesus Christ lives in you, you yourself can be born into this very family, the same family as Jesus, as one of the immortal, divine children of God.

There. I said it. I know it may sound strange or hyperbolic to many people, including some longtime Christians who may have never seen it put that way before, but the Bible itself makes it abundantly clear that the divine family of God is having children—many children, in fact—all of whom are meant to become something infinitely greater than we are now greater, even, than angels.

Scripture refers to God's obedient people as "the children of God," who will become "partakers of the divine nature," endowed with and sharing the glory of Christ, elevated above the angels to judge angels and the citizens of this world, who will rule and reign alongside their literal brother Jesus, and even sit down on the very throne of the Creator of the universe. Your own Bible already says all this, and I'm going to show you where, so it's no longer an unexplained mystery.

You've already seen part of this text, but here now is the complete thought on the matter addressed by the apostle Paul:

> God has given me the responsibility of serving his church by proclaiming his entire message to you.

> This message was kept secret for centuries and generations past, but now it has been revealed to God's people. For God wanted them to know that the riches and glory of Christ are for you Gentiles, too. And THIS IS THE SECRET: CHRIST LIVES IN YOU. THIS GIVES YOU ASSURANCE OF SHARING HIS GLORY. (Colossians 1:25-27 NLT, emphasis added)

And WHY has the secret been revealed? It's so everyone can believe and obey God:

> The message about Christ is the secret that was hidden for long ages past but is now made known. It has been made clear through the writings of the prophets. And by the command of the eternal God it is made known to all nations that they might believe and obey. (Romans 16:25-26 NCV)

The divine secret, you see, is, in reality, an open secret about your mind-boggling, glorious destiny. Unfortunately, it hasn't been proclaimed enough throughout the world. However, God has indicated that in the end time, "knowledge shall be increased" (Daniel 12:4 KJV). So, if we're living in the end time or close to it, many more people will finally have their minds opened to the secret of the Good News that was hidden from everyone since the beginning of time.

The Children of God

When people consider the idea of having children, I'd venture to say most probably think it's not such a big deal. After all, humans have been giving birth to their own offspring for thousands of years now. Even looking at the animal kingdom, horses have been giving birth to horses, cats have been giving birth to cats, and giraffes have been plopping out giraffes, for ages. Everything reproduces, having offspring after its own kind, just the way it was meant to be. Now, believe it or not, God is also producing offspring.

As we've seen, members of the God family decided to reproduce after Their own kind, after Their own likeness. Unfortunately, many people are simply unaware that the New Testament clearly says we're the *offspring of God*:

> ... for in Him we live and move and have our being, as also some of your own poets have said, "For we are also His offspring." Therefore, SINCE WE ARE THE OFFSPRING OF GOD, we ought not to think that the Divine Nature is like gold or silver or stone, something shaped by art and man's devising. (Acts 17:28-29 NKJV, emphasis added)

Yes, we're the offspring of the divine Creator. So says the Bible. But the more common phrases found in Scripture regarding the reason we're all here are "children of God" and "sons of God." You'll probably recognize many of these verses as we examine them in a variety of translations, and as you see the words on the page, remember that God is outright telling you your intended destiny each time.

> Blessed are the peacemakers: for they shall be called the children of God. (Matthew 5:9 KJV)
>
> For as many as are led by the Spirit of God, these are sons of God. (Romans 8:14 NKJV)
>
> The Spirit itself beareth witness with our spirit, that we are the children of God ... (Romans 8:16 KJV)
>
> But to all who did accept him and believe in him he gave the right to become children of God. (John 1:12 NCV)

> . . . so that you may become blameless and pure, children of God without fault in a crooked and depraved generation, in which you shine like stars in the universe . . . (Philippians 2:15 NIV)

> For you are all sons of God through faith in Christ Jesus. (Galatians 3:26 NKJV)

> "I will be your father, and you will be my sons and daughters, says the Lord Almighty." (2 Corinthians 6:18 NCV)

> The Father has loved us so much that we are called children of God. And we really are his children. (1 John 3:1 NCV)

There are many more verses which contain the terms "children of God" and "sons of God" in the Bible, and we'll take a look at them as we continue, but I just wanted to start off with a few obvious ones so you could see the Bible has little problem declaring what we are, and are intended to be. We're not low life forms such as bacteria, mosquitoes, or worms. Though we came from the ground, we're not daisies, wheat, cotton, or trees. We're not domesticated pets like parakeets, goldfish, hamsters, dogs, or cats. We're not the great animals of the wild such as deer, bears, tigers, or whales. We're not even angels or destined to become angels. We are something unique in all of creation, something called the *children of God*. God is having kids, and as we've just read in John 1:12, "to all who did accept him and believe in him he gave the right to become children of God."

Now at this point, you might be thinking to yourself, *Wait a second. Am I an actual child of God right now? Am I a member of the God family? After all, I can't walk through walls too easily, at least not without getting my head bashed apart.*

That's an excellent point, and it sits at the very heart of the divine secret. Although the Bible declares obedient believers to be part of God's very own family, all of the tremendous abilities and benefits of being in the God family are not immediately visible and available just yet. There's a waiting period before everything takes effect, because God is completing us in stages. We're sort of like a prototype now. Here's how John put it: "Dear friends, now we are children of God, and we have not yet been shown what we will be in the future." (1 John 3:2 NCV)

Read those words again, and notice that even though right now we are the children of God, it also says we have not yet been shown what we're going to be in the future. In other words, at some point in the days ahead, we're going to become something much greater than our mortal, flesh-and-blood bodies allow us to be at the present time. A staggering metamorphosis is to come.

When precisely will this happen? And just what will we become? The rest of that very same verse answers the questions for us: "But we know that when Christ comes again, we will be like him, because we will see him as he really is." (1 John 3:2 NCV)

This is one of the most revealing lines in all of Scripture. First of all, it specifies the moment that things really change for the better. It says "when Christ comes again." It's referring to what is commonly called today "the Second Coming of Jesus Christ."

For those who aren't Bible aficionados, Jesus (the Word) left His dwelling place in heaven approximately two thousand years ago to live here on Earth among His own people He had created thousands of years earlier.

He spoke of this shortly before He was put to death: "I came forth from the Father and have come into the world. Again, I leave the world and go to the Father." (John 16:28 NKJV)

God the Father then raised Jesus from the dead, and brought Him back to heaven, where Jesus was glorified and now reigns, "sitting at the right hand of God" as we've read, preparing to come back at some point in the future. In fact, the very people who personally witnessed Jesus floating up to heaven were told that He'd be returning once again to Earth: "This same Jesus, who was taken up from you into heaven, will so come in like manner as you saw Him go into heaven." (Acts 1:11 NKJV)

There's much more on that coming later. What I wish to focus on now is that "when Christ comes again, we will be like him, because we will see him as he really is." Your very own Bible says upon Jesus' return to Earth, we're going to be LIKE HIM. We're actually going to be like Jesus! On His level! And we'll see Him as He really is, in all His brightly shining, divine glory! How is this possible? Because just as the Bible says, we're going to be like Him. Immortal. Glorified. Made of spirit. No longer flesh and blood. Members of the actual God family. Brothers and sisters of Christ. Children of God.

This is a huge newsflash for many people, even for some who have been sitting through countless sermons for decades, because so few people ever want to step near the verses that talk about the divine secret. But they're the most fascinating and revealing of all the portions of Scripture. Again, the Bible says what it means: We're going to be like Jesus when He comes again.

It may be difficult for some to think the Bible truly says we're meant to be in the same divine family as God, all glorified brothers of Jesus, but these words are plastered all over your own Bible, and I want you to see them with your own eyes right now.

In the book of Hebrews, we read:

> Jesus, who makes people holy, and those who are made holy are from the same family. So he is not ashamed to call them his brothers and sisters. He

says, "Then, I will tell my brothers and sisters about you; I will praise you in the public meeting." He also says, "I will trust in God." And he also says, "I am here, and with me are the children God has given me." (Hebrews 2:11-13 NCV)

Right at the very start, this portion of Scripture proudly repeats what we've seen before—that God is a family. Not only that, but it says both Jesus and those who are made holy—that is to say, His obedient followers—"are from the same family." Are you getting that? We're from the exact same family as God. It's no wonder the very next sentence says Jesus is not ashamed to call them His very own brothers and sisters. Yes, the family terms of brothers and sisters are used, because faithful men and women are destined to become just what the Bible says—the actual, real-life brothers and sisters of Jesus Christ, their fellow member of the God family.

Let's look again at the verses discussing a family in heaven: "For this reason I bow my knees to the Father of our Lord Jesus Christ, from whom the whole family in heaven and earth is named" (Ephesians 3:14-15 NKJV).

As previously stated, this Scripture clearly tells us there's a "family in heaven." But it tells us more. It refers to the "whole family in heaven and earth," and says that this entire family is named for our Father in heaven. I don't want you to overlook the significance of what the Bible is saying here. Members of God's own family are not only in heaven, but right here on Planet Earth right now, because believers are given the right to be children of God, though they have not yet been raised from the dead to an immortal and glorified state.

Jesus Christ has already been glorified as a member of the divine family of God. The Bible sums that up by indicating, "Christ was chosen before the world was made, but he was shown to the world in these last times for your sake. Through Christ you believe in God, who raised Christ from the dead and gave him glory." (1 Peter 1:20-21 NCV)

But what many people either overlook or just have never heard before is that Jesus is not the only one meant to be glorified by God. There are others—plenty of others. Paul states that Jesus is merely "the firstborn among many brothers and sisters." (Romans 8:29 NLT)

Hebrews 2:10 indicates that God is "bringing many sons to glory" (NKJV). MANY sons. Not just one. A whole bunch. The New Century Version translates the same verse by saying, "He wanted to have many children share his glory . . . ." Are you hearing what the Bible is shouting? God is looking to have MANY sons. MANY children SHARE HIS GLORY.

This incredible theme—of children of God receiving and sharing the same glory that Jesus was given—is mentioned constantly throughout the New Testament. Here's a sampling:

> Christ is your life, and when he comes again, you will share in his glory. (Colossians 3:4 NCV)

> And I, too, will share his glory and his honor when he returns. (1 Peter 5:1 NLT)

> And when the Chief Shepherd appears, you will receive the crown of glory that does not fade away. (1 Peter 5:4 NKJV)

> For I consider that the sufferings of this present time are not worthy to be compared with the glory which shall be revealed in us. (Romans 8:18 NKJV)

> We have small troubles for a while now, but they are helping us gain an eternal glory that is much greater than the troubles. (2 Corinthians 4:17 NCV)

...the eyes of your understanding being enlightened;
that you may know what is the hope of His calling,
what are the riches of the glory of His inheritance
in the saints ... (Ephesians 1:18 NKJV)

For God wanted them to know that the riches and
glory of Christ are for you Gentiles, too. And this
is the secret: Christ lives in you. This gives you
assurance of sharing his glory. (Colossians 1:27
NLT)

And, just in case you haven't seen enough proof yet, get a load
of this from Paul:

I speak God's secret wisdom, which he has kept
hidden. Before the world began, God planned this
wisdom **for our glory**. None of the rulers of this
world understood it. **If they had, they would not
have crucified the Lord of glory.** (1 Corinthians
2:7-8 NCV, emphasis added)

Again, Paul brought up the secret knowledge which was
conceived before the world began, and which God kept under
wraps. But in this brief portion of Scripture, he answered the
question about why it was planned. He said God devised the
secret wisdom FOR OUR GLORY. Because God has intended for
us to be glorified and to share in the same glory that Christ has
received. Our destiny is beyond breathtaking.

And as mentioned before, Paul stressed that if this hidden
knowledge had been fully understood by the powers in charge
when Jesus was performing miracles, He never would have been
crucified! If the people of Jesus' day were fully aware of His identity
as the divine Creator who made the first man out of the ground,
the one who said "Let there be light," the one who spoke to Moses
face to face, and the one who created people to eventually become
divine children of God, they would never have dared to slay Him.

That's Just Divine

I know I've said a lot in the previous few pages, but just in case you missed the best part about the divine secret, here it is again: The family of God is having many children, and when Jesus Christ lives in you, you yourself can be born into this very family—the same family as Jesus—as one of the immortal, divine children of God.

Now, you might be thinking to yourself, "Sure, I can go along with being immortal, because the Bible so often talks about eternal life or everlasting life. But what about this *divine* business? Will I actually partake of the divine nature?"

In a word, yes, and the Bible says so, using that exact phrase. It's found in the New Testament, where the apostle by the name of Simon Peter talked about some "exceedingly great and precious promises," that we'll be "partakers of the divine nature." Here it is:

> "Grace and peace be multiplied to you in the knowledge of God and of Jesus our Lord, as His divine power has given to us all things that pertain to life and godliness, through the knowledge of Him who called us by glory and virtue, by which have been given to us exceedingly great and precious promises, that through these YOU MAY BE PARTAKERS OF THE DIVINE NATURE, having escaped the corruption that is in the world through lust." (2 Peter 1:2-4 NKJV, emphasis added)

It's not just one translation that says we can partake of God's divine nature. The King James Version says, "exceeding great and precious promises: that by these ye might be partakers of the divine nature . . ."

The New International Version mentions "very great and precious promises, so that through them you may participate in the divine nature . . ."

And the New Living translation declares: "And because of his glory and excellence, he has given us great and precious promises. These are the promises that enable you to share his divine nature ..."

The Bible means what it says, folks. The divine secret reveals exceedingly great and precious promises—promises that are so great and precious, your own mind may not even want to accept them at first. It is not too good to be true. Scripture states unequivocally that we're meant to partake, participate in, and share the divine nature, the actual divine nature that God our Father and Jesus Christ already share. If people would just crack open their own Bibles and read the words on the page, they might finally understand the mind-blowing, sensational reward the God family has designated for the sons and daughters of God!

This partaking of the divine nature is expressed in different ways in the Bible, including becoming "filled with all the fullness of God."

In Ephesians 3:19, we read, "to know the love of Christ which passes knowledge; that you may be filled with all the fullness of God." (NKJV) Once again, this is merely a matter of reading the words that are printed, because they tell us exactly what is meant for us.

It says we're going to be filled with something, and that something is the most awesome thing that could ever be offered to us, and that is "the fullness of God." In other words, we are going to be full members of the very family of God, on the same divine plane, filled with the very same attributes and abilities that God the Father and Jesus possess. For starters, that means becoming immortal, never having to die again once we've been resurrected. As Paul termed it, "eternal life to those who by patient continuance in doing good seek for glory, honor, and immortality." (Romans 2:7 NKJV)

Another way our future divine nature is discussed is quite possibly the most stunning portion in all of Scripture, and it's found in both the Old and New Testaments, and even being spoken by Jesus Christ. It first occurs in Psalm 82:6, which reads:

> I said, "You are gods, And all of you are children of
> the Most High." (NKJV)

You're not misreading that. Those are the words on the pages of the Bible. Look it up in your own version, and then another version, and then another. God's own Holy Word says that you are gods, and that all of you are children of the Most High. It's not a mistranslation, because the word that is rendered as "gods" in English is *Elohim* in Hebrew, the same exact word used for *God* in Genesis, when the God family is first mentioned.

Remember, *Elohim* is a *plural* word, and this amazing verse again confirms the divine secret: We are designed as children of the Most High. God is actually having kids, and we're the offspring of the divine God! I must stress that this does NOT indicate we become God the Father or Jesus Christ, or that we somehow become superior to Them. They are Their own, original, distinctly individual members of the God family and will always remain in charge over everything, including us:

> Then, when all things are under his authority, the
> Son will put himself under God's authority, so that
> God, who gave his Son authority over all things, will
> be utterly supreme over everything everywhere. (1
> Corinthians 15:28 NLT)

But it does mean exactly what it says, that we're the children of the Most High God, all part of the same God family.

Jesus Himself directly referred to this concept in the New Testament, when He was being harassed by religious leaders while walking through the temple during a winter visit. Here's the account in its entire context, so you can see for yourself that Jesus meant exactly what was said in the Old Testament:

> Then the Jews surrounded Him and said to Him, "How long do You keep us in doubt? If You are the Christ, tell us plainly." Jesus answered them, "I told you, and you do not believe. The works that I do in My Father's name, they bear witness of Me. But you do not believe, because you are not of My sheep, as I said to you. My sheep hear My voice, and I know them, and they follow Me. And I give them eternal life, and they shall never perish; neither shall anyone snatch them out of My hand. My Father, who has given them to Me, is greater than all; and no one is able to snatch them out of My Father's hand. I and My Father are one."

> Then the Jews took up stones again to stone Him. Jesus answered them, "Many good works I have shown you from My Father. For which of those works do you stone Me?" The Jews answered Him, saying, "For a good work we do not stone You, but for blasphemy, and because You, being a Man, make Yourself God."

> Jesus answered them, "Is it not written in your law, 'I said, "You are gods"'? If He called them gods, to whom the word of God came (and the Scripture cannot be broken), do you say of Him whom the Father sanctified and sent into the world, 'You are blaspheming,' because I said, 'I am the Son of God'? (John 10:24-36 NKJV)

This exchange is nothing short of stupendous, and is filled with plenty of eye-opening information. So just in case you haven't been paying attention up till now, it's time to wake up and focus big-time.

First of all, this man Jesus—who, again, is really the divine member of the God family who personally created everything—confirmed that He is the "Christ," which is the Greek word for *Messiah*, literally meaning "Anointed One." He is the Savior.

"I told you, and you do not believe," is how He answered the Jews who demanded an answer if He indeed were the Christ. But the information gets even more revealing. Jesus said He Himself is one who personally imparts eternal life to obedient human beings:

> "I give them eternal life, and they shall never perish."
> (v. 28)

Jesus informed everyone right at that moment that He is, in fact, God! He's a member of the divine *Elohim*, the family of God, and He bestows immortality on people He calls His sheep. He goes on to say that "I and My Father are one." Once again, He's reminding us of the real beginning, the very first verse of the gospel of John which talks about the Word being with God, and the Word was God. Jesus (the Word) and the Father are both God. Both are members of the one God family, and they do things in singular harmony with each other.

But still, there's so much more to this scene. The Jews understood exactly what Jesus was saying about Himself. They understood His declaration that He was indeed God, a member of the divine family. They admitted it when Jesus asked them why they wanted to kill Him by pummeling Him with rocks:

> "For a good work we do not stone You, but for blasphemy, and because You, being a Man, make Yourself God." (v. 33)

The response from Jesus to their statement is as fascinating as it is fantastic. He could have said something to the effect of, "Yes, you're right, I am indeed God. In fact, I'm the one who created all of you to begin with, starting with Adam, when I scooped up a pile of dirt and breathed life into his nostrils."

But He said something much more intriguing. It was a response that again reveals and confirms the divine secret.

> Jesus answered them, "Is it not written in your law, 'I said, "You are gods"'? If He called them gods, to whom the word of God came (and the Scripture cannot be broken), do you say of Him whom the Father sanctified and sent into the world, 'You are blaspheming,' because I said, 'I am the Son of God'? (vv. 34 36)

Let's take a very close look at these striking words on the page. First of all, Jesus appealed to the law that was already on the books, the Old Testament Scripture of Psalm 82:6. He didn't mention the specific chapter and verse, because the Bible had not yet been divided up into chapters and verses. But He cited their own Scripture which quoted the Creator and stated, "I said, 'You are gods.'"

For those wondering about the New Testament Greek word translated here as "gods," it is *Theos*, the exact same word that's used when referring to the divine God, such as God the Father.

Jesus continued the analysis and said if the Creator God (in other words, Himself during Old Testament times) called those people "gods," and everyone knows that Scripture can't be broken, then why are you accusing Me (Jesus) of blasphemy because I said I'm the Son of God?

A more modern way of putting it might sound like: "Uh, hello, people?! It's already written in your own unbreakable law that God has called YOU YOURSELVES *gods*. So why on Earth are you getting on my case just because I call myself God's Son?"

Jesus let these so-called religious leaders know that they didn't even understand their own Scripture. The Creator of the universe had already declared in unbreakable Scripture that human beings are *gods*, all children of the Most High God! This is our destiny! It is what we were designed to be from the beginning. In your own Bible, God has already called us ELOHIM, the Hebrew word for the God family. In your own Bible, God has already called us THEOS, the Greek word for God. In your own Bible, God has already called us *gods!* Remember, the children of cats are cats. The children of dogs are dogs. And the children of God are—say it with me, folks—*gods!* The one God family is meant to get very big with *many* children of God! Read it for yourself! Highlight it. Think about it. If you're not still getting it, pray about it, and ask your Creator to open your mind to this tremendous truth.

As we revisit what Paul said about the divine secret, let's read more of his thoughts for a glimpse of how magnificent the future is going to be:

> As I briefly wrote earlier, God himself revealed his mysterious plan to me. As you read what I have written, you will understand my insight into this plan regarding Christ. God did not reveal it to previous generations, but now by his Spirit he has revealed it to his holy apostles and prophets. And this is God's plan: Both Gentiles and Jews who believe the Good News share equally in the riches inherited by God's children. Both are part of the same body, and both enjoy the promise of blessings because they belong to Christ Jesus. (Ephesians 3:3-6 NLT)

Yes, everyone who was ever born, no matter what race, ethnicity, or nation they're born into, can partake in the riches inherited by God's children, because they will be the actual children of God, in the same body—that is, the same family of God. Paul indicated this plan is virtually impossible for our minds to fully conceive:

> No, the wisdom we speak of is the mystery of God—his plan that was previously hidden, even though he made it for our ultimate glory before the world began. But the rulers of this world have not understood it; if they had, they would not have crucified our glorious Lord. That is what the Scriptures mean when they say,
>
> > "No eye has seen, no ear has heard,
> > and no mind has imagined
> > what God has prepared
> > for those who love him."
>
> But it was to us that God revealed these things by his Spirit. For his Spirit searches out everything and shows us God's deep secrets. (1 Corinthians 2:7-10 NLT)

Over and over again, your Bible talks about God's deep secrets, saying God has prepared things which our eyes have not seen and our ears have not heard, things which have not entered into people's hearts. But they're no longer mysterious. They've been revealed to us by the Spirit of God, the very mind and power of the God family.

The Creator of the universe, Jesus Christ, has engraved the divine secret in Holy Scripture in open terms, where it's there for all eyes to see, if people would just read the words on the page. We are indeed the children of God, the literal offspring of the divine family, and we all have the potential of being partakers of the divine nature, becoming immortal members of the actual family of God!

Chapter 2

The Quickening

Behold, I tell you a mystery: We shall not all sleep, but we shall all be changed . . . (1 Corinthians 15:51 NKJV)

Now that you've been introduced to the meaning of the divine secret, it's time to delve deeper into this "mystery," as the Bible calls it, regarding our outstanding destiny and how and when it all takes place. It's some of the most intriguing and enthralling information that God has provided us, but it rarely seems to get mentioned in church or in general public discussion. So let's see what the Bible itself has to say and savor the delicious details.

Without trying to sound like political campaigns of recent years, there's change coming. A big change. It's a change that will completely transform the lives of anyone who is a true follower of God. I'm not referring to any change of course in your life, such as changing your attitude, changing your mind, changing your college major, changing your job, changing the TV channel or changing your underwear. I'm not even talking about stopping idiotic behavior in order to live a kinder, gentler, more decent kind of life. I'm talking about a fundamental transformation in your actual make-up, the ingredients in your body that you carry around every day.

Part of the mystery of the divine secret is the fact that our human, physical bodies are designed to be changed by God in an almost unfathomable way. There's a monumental metamorphosis coming that will completely transform our bodies, far more than shedding a lot of weight. But exactly what's going to happen? And how long does the process take? We don't need to make guesses, because the Bible actually provides the answers.

There's a unique word used in the King James Version of the Bible to describe this awesome change event. That word is "quicken." To "quicken" literally means to make alive, to cause to live. It's an injection of life, and most of the time when it's used in the Bible, it refers to the eternal, immortal life so often promised, though not guaranteed, in Scripture.

We need that injection of life because we're not already immortal. We're mortal, physical beings who will die unless given immortal life by God. In case you've never seen or heard this verse before (and I can't imagine that most people haven't because it's plastered all over countless sports events including football quarterback Tim Tebow's face), the most famous line of the Bible is John 3:16, which talks about two opposites: perishing vs. everlasting life: "For God so loved the world that He gave His only begotten Son, that whoever believes in Him should not perish but have everlasting life." (NKJV)

Again, this line lets us know that if we don't believe in Jesus and follow Him, we can expect to perish. And we all know what "perish" means. It means having no life, utter destruction, being dead forever. Psalm 73:27 states plainly: "Those who are far from you will perish; you destroy all who are unfaithful to you." (NIV) But the verse in John also tells us that if we do accept Jesus, we can be alive forever, enjoying the reward of everlasting, eternal, immortal life, however you wish to say it.

Biblically speaking, the moment we acquire eternal life is known as getting quickened. Here's an excellent verse describing the change:

> But if the Spirit of him that raised up Jesus from the dead dwell in you, he that raised up Christ from the dead shall also quicken your mortal bodies by his Spirit that dwelleth in you. (Romans 8:11 KJV)

If you're not understanding the sense of what "quicken" means yet, here's the same verse from the New Living Translation:

> The Spirit of God, who raised Jesus from the dead, lives in you. And just as God raised Christ Jesus from the dead, he will give life to your mortal bodies by this same Spirit living within you.

Quickening your mortal bodies is translated here simply and accurately as giving life to your mortal bodies. It means to make your perishable bodies immortal, to receive everlasting life instead of just a temporary existence like the one we have right now. Again, I need to stress that people are not immortal already. There's nowhere in the Bible that says any part of you is immortal; in fact, the Bible goes out of its way to say that human beings are presently mortal, as in the following verses, with emphasis added:

> For this corruptible must put on incorruption, and this MORTAL must PUT ON IMMORTALITY. (1 Corinthians 15:53 NKJV)

> Therefore do not let sin reign in your MORTAL body, that you should obey it in its lusts. (Romans 6:12 NKJV)

> For the wages of sin is DEATH, but the gift of God is eternal life in Christ Jesus our Lord. (Romans 6:23 NKJV)

Yes, all of us are currently sinful, mortal beings headed for everlasting death if we don't repent, but the gift of God is eternal life, and we can actually "put on immortality" if we're faithful to God. It's basic and self-explanatory. But let's get back to the quickening, the moment when we change from mortal to immortal.

The concept is talked about in both the Old and New Testaments quite a bit. In the King James Version of Psalm 119, for instance, the word "quicken" is used eleven times in its present or past tense, including:

> Behold, I have longed after thy precepts: quicken me in thy righteousness. (v. 40)

> Great are thy tender mercies, O LORD: quicken me according to thy judgments. (v. 156)

In the New Testament, the Q-word is also used often:

> For Christ also hath once suffered for sins, the just for the unjust, that he might bring us to God, being put to death in the flesh, but quickened by the Spirit. (1 Peter 3:18 KJV)

Notice how the Bible uses the term, saying Jesus was put to death in his physical, flesh-and-blood body, but then quickened— that is to say, made immortally alive—by the Spirit.

In John 6:63, we're told by Jesus, "It is the spirit that quickeneth; the flesh profiteth nothing." A more modern translation makes it a little clearer: "It is the Spirit that gives life. The flesh doesn't give life." (NCV)

This is another way of the Bible saying what we already know, that we as flesh-and-blood human beings are mortal. There is no eternal life inherent in our current bodies. We need the Spirit of God inside us to quicken us—to enable us to make the transition from mortal to immortal.

Here's another interesting tidbit about being quickened:

> For as the Father raiseth up the dead, and quickeneth them; even so the Son quickeneth whom he will. (John 5:21 KJV)

> Just as the Father raises the dead and gives them life, so also the Son gives life to those he wants to. (NCV)

Here we're informed of something that harks back to the different members of God's family, and it clearly says that God the Father has the ability to raise dead people from their graves and make them immortal, but Jesus also has that very same ability and can quicken anyone He chooses to everlasting life. Jesus Himself is even referred to as "a quickening spirit," meaning an immortality-giving spirit, in 1 Corinthians 15:45 (KJV).

The Ingredients

Now that we're clear on the fact that our big change involves a quickening from mortal to immortal, we can look at another major part of the mystery, and that has to do with the actual components of our body. What are we made of at present, and what are we going to become?

Right now, as most of us realize, we are made up of physical matter, often referred to as flesh and blood. We all have muscles, bones, tendons, nerves, blood, and water inside of us. The bodily ingredients that make up our flesh and blood are all composed of elements on the periodic table, such as carbon, oxygen, and hydrogen, all of which are materials found here on this planet. Remember, God created Adam from the ground itself, so it makes perfect sense that human beings consist of much of the same matter found throughout the Earth.

The word "flesh" is found scores of times throughout Scripture and often refers to our physical bodies, as is seen when the term is used for the very first time, when God was creating the first woman, Eve, from the flesh of Adam:

> And the LORD God caused a deep sleep to fall on Adam, and he slept; and He took one of his ribs, and closed up the flesh in its place. Then the rib which the LORD God had taken from man He made into a woman, and He brought her to the man. And Adam said: "This is now bone of my bones And flesh of my flesh . . . " (Genesis 2:21-23 NKJV)

Yes, all human beings consist of flesh. But it may surprise you that we're not meant to be made out of flesh forever. This is part of the great mystery of God's plan for His children. You and I are designed to undergo a phenomenal change, the spectacular quickening to be composed of something else. And that something else is another substance, a substance which is not made of any physical matter. There are no protons, neutrons, or electrons in this substance. No atoms and no molecules, either. It's the exact same stuff of which God is comprised. And that, as we've already seen, is spirit.

Remember, the Bible says that "God is Spirit." (John 4:24 NKJV) And since we human beings are going to become the actual children of God, then we, ourselves, will be changed into spirit-composed bodies as well, looking very much like the glorified body of the Creator of the universe, Jesus Christ.

We're directly informed of this in the New Testament, when it refers to Jesus and the action He'll be taking with us: "By his power to rule all things, he will change our humble bodies and make them like his own glorious body." (Philippians 3:21 NCV)

Once again, Scripture is talking about the striking change, the quickening, the transformation of our current, mortal, physical, flesh-and-blood bodies into a body that indeed resembles the "glorious body" of Jesus. We're gonna look like Jesus, folks. And as we've read in the previous chapter, Jesus' body at the present time is not looking flayed apart and bloody as it did during His execution. It's been cleaned up, quickened by God the Father, and glorified into an awesome sight that impressed John when he saw Jesus in a vision while the apostle was living on the Aegean Sea island of Patmos late in the first century:

> His head and hair were white like wool, as white as
> snow, and his eyes were like flames of fire. His feet
> were like bronze that glows hot in a furnace, and
> his voice was like the noise of flooding water. . . .
> He looked like the sun shining at its brightest time.
> (Revelation 1:14-16 NCV)

This is what Jesus looks like right now! He's not hanging on a cross or stake any longer with ribs exposed and chunks of his beard ripped from his face. Remember, Jesus is the Word, the creating agent of God's family, and God's family is not composed of flesh and blood, but spirit. Our bodies are meant to undergo the exact same transformation that Jesus did, from bodies consisting of flesh and blood to bodies consisting of spirit:

> "Beloved, now we are children of God; and it has
> not yet been revealed what we shall be, but we know
> that when He is revealed, we shall be like Him, for
> we shall see Him as He is." (1 John 3:2 NKJV)

We're going to be LIKE HIM—just like Jesus is! But it simply has not been revealed yet, because we still haven't been quickened out of these mortal bodies into our immortal ones.

Now, how can we be so sure that we're going to have our physical, flesh-and-blood bodies changed into spirit-composed bodies? I mean, isn't there a possibility that we could enter God's own kingdom, the very family of God, with flesh-and-blood bodies that just happened to be quickened into flesh-and-blood bodies that become immortal? This is an excellent question, and certainly one which can't be overlooked.

The answer is actually quite simple, because the Bible tells us in no uncertain terms that people who make it into the kingdom of God will no longer be made up of flesh and blood. Here's one of those Bible verses you should highlight and memorize:

> Now this I say, brethren, that flesh and blood cannot inherit the kingdom of God. (1 Corinthians 15:50 NKJV)

It doesn't matter which version of the Bible you're reading. All translations convey the same idea, with just slightly different wording:

> I tell you this, brothers and sisters: Flesh and blood cannot have a part in the kingdom of God. (NCV)

> What I am saying, dear brothers and sisters, is that our physical bodies cannot inherit the Kingdom of God. (NLT)

Once again, the Bible means exactly what it says. Our physical bodies, which currently consist of a skeleton covered with muscles, tendons, and skin, with blood coursing through arteries and veins in an extensive and complex circulatory system, will not be members of the coming kingdom of God. They'll first have to undergo the change. The quickening from mortality to immortality. The transformation from flesh and blood into spirit. We'll actually have to be born again into our brand-new spirit bodies.

Born of the Spirit

That brings us to one of the most fascinating and revealing conversations in the entire Bible, one that directly addresses this very subject. It's found in the third chapter of the gospel of John (yes, the same chapter with the most famous line of the Bible— John 3:16), and it's a discussion between Jesus and a religious leader of the day named Nicodemus. Before analyzing it in detail, please read it for yourself uninterrupted, so you can get the flow of the conversation:

> There was a man of the Pharisees named Nicodemus, a ruler of the Jews.
>
> This man came to Jesus by night and said to Him, "Rabbi, we know that You are a teacher come from God; for no one can do these signs that You do unless God is with him."
>
> Jesus answered and said to him, "Most assuredly, I say to you, unless one is born again, he cannot see the kingdom of God."
>
> Nicodemus said to Him, "How can a man be born when he is old? Can he enter a second time into his mother's womb and be born?"
>
> Jesus answered, "Most assuredly, I say to you, unless one is born of water and the Spirit, he cannot enter the kingdom of God. That which is born of the flesh is flesh, and that which is born of the Spirit is spirit. Do not marvel that I said to you, 'You must be born again.' The wind blows where it wishes, and you hear the sound of it, but cannot tell where it comes from and where it goes. So is everyone who is born of the Spirit."
>
> Nicodemus answered and said to Him, "How can these things be?"
>
> Jesus answered and said to him, "Are you the teacher of Israel, and do not know these things?

> Most assuredly, I say to you, We speak what We know and testify what We have seen, and you do not receive Our witness. If I have told you earthly things and you do not believe, how will you believe if I tell you heavenly things? (John 3:1-12 NKJV)

According to John, Nicodemus was a Pharisee, one of the rulers of the Jewish people at the time, and he came to see Jesus at night. Perhaps this is just speculation, but it's possible Nicodemus traveled under the cover of darkness because he didn't want his fellow Pharisees to find out that he was visiting this controversial guy named Jesus. The Pharisees were not fans of Jesus, and most of them wanted Him dead. They constantly plotted to kill Him, and eventually paid Judas Iscariot, one of Jesus' own apostles, thirty pieces of silver to betray the Savior.

But Nicodemus made a startling admission at the outset of his conversation. When calling Jesus "Rabbi" (meaning teacher), he acknowledged, "we know that You are a teacher come from God; for no one can do these signs that You do unless God is with him."

This had to strike Jesus' interest. Here was a member of an opposing religious crowd possibly risking his own life by coming to see Jesus. Nicodemus admitted that they KNEW Jesus was a teacher come from God, and they were well aware God had to be with Jesus for Him to be performing all the miraculous signs, such as healing the blind and lame, and even raising some dead people back to physical life.

Jesus, realizing that he was talking to someone who was aware of at least that basic truth, decided to steer the discussion immediately to the intended future destiny, the quickening, that moment when people are transformed into their spirit-composed bodies. He started off by calling it being "born again."

"Most assuredly, I say to you, unless one is born again, he cannot see the kingdom of God." (v. 3)

Jesus said exactly what He meant—that human beings are designed to undergo a second process of birth—and Nicodemus understood that's what Jesus was getting at. But it apparently left him a bit puzzled, because he followed up with this question: "How can a man be born when he is old? Can he enter a second time into his mother's womb and be born?"

Jesus answered by explaining there's a jump that needs to be made from our mortal, human bodies consisting of flesh into our glorious, immortal, quickened bodies that will be made up of spirit: "That which is born of the flesh is flesh, and that which is born of the Spirit is spirit." (v. 6)

Look at this sentence again, and read it slowly: "That which is born of the flesh is flesh, and that which is born of the Spirit is spirit."

Many people who read the Bible don't realize the crystal clear truth being declared by Jesus. He's saying that whatever offspring is born of flesh, whether human or animal, is also going to consist of flesh. You already know this without being told. Horses give birth to flesh-and-blood horses. The offspring of lions are flesh-and-blood lions. And human beings give birth to flesh-and-blood human beings.

But He goes on to state something else, something less obvious but far more profound: "That which is born of the Spirit is spirit."

Jesus was saying that whatever offspring is born of the Spirit (remember, God is Spirit) is also going to consist of spirit! The very same substance that comprises God! That's why flesh and blood cannot inherit or be part of the kingdom of God. When we're born into the actual family of God as children of God, we'll become spirit-composed beings just like God the Father and Jesus.

The conversation didn't end there, though. Jesus continued, "Do not marvel that I said to you, 'You must be born again.' The wind blows where it wishes, and you hear the sound of it, but cannot tell where it comes from and where it goes. So is everyone who is born of the Spirit." (vv. 7-8)

He told Nicodemus not to be surprised by this idea of being born for a second time, being quickened into a body that is actually comprised of spirit instead of physical matter. He compared it to the wind, which blows in any given direction, but is completely invisible to our human, physical, flesh-and-blood eyes. The effects of the wind can be seen and heard, such as pine needles whispering, leaves rustling, and limbs bending, but the wind itself is hidden from normal view. He said it's a similar situation for people, once they're born for a second time into their spirit bodies. They're on a whole different plateau of existence. It starts with invisibility to things that are physical. People will have finally reached the spirit plane—the level of God's family as children of God.

Hearing all this spectacular truth was a bit mind-rattling for Nicodemus to handle, and he asked Jesus, "How can these things be?"

It's very interesting to note the response of Jesus. He didn't continue to explain in a calm, cool, methodical fashion more revelatory information about the process of becoming quickened into a spirit body. Instead, somewhat incredulous at Nicodemus' ignorance, He proceeded to insult the Jewish leader: "Are you the teacher of Israel, and do not know these things?" (v. 10)

He wondered how Nicodemus could even be called "the teacher of Israel" if he were in the dark about such important matters. He should have known them because as a learned instructor, he was intended to understand God's fantastic plan, the divine secret revealed to his prophets many years prior.

Jesus concluded the discussion by saying, "If I have told you earthly things and you do not believe, how will you believe if I tell you heavenly things?" (v. 12)

Jesus continued his verbal slam of Nicodemus for not knowing the stated plan of God, for not understanding that human beings are meant to be quickened, to undergo an actual second birth, not a birth into a body made of flesh, but a birth into a body made of spirit. Nicodemus just didn't get it, as many religious leaders today still don't get it. Jesus clearly said that whatever is born of the Spirit is actually spirit! It's no longer made of physical matter. It's composed of spirit. It consists of spirit. It's made up of spirit. The ingredients on the label of our new bodies will be 100 percent spirit!

The Changing

For the place in the Bible that best sums up the quickening from mortality to immortality and the transformation from bodies made of flesh to bodies made of spirit, look at the fifteenth chapter of the book of Corinthians.

Again, I'll provide you a chunk of text so you can read it in its own context without commercial interruption, and then I'll take you through its key points so you don't miss any of the stunning revelations. I've selected the New Living Translation for this section just because of its ease of readability, but I encourage you to read it in any and all translations, including your favorite, because the message is the same no matter which Bible version you select:

> But someone may ask, "How will the dead be raised? What kind of bodies will they have?" What a foolish question! When you put a seed into the ground, it doesn't grow into a plant unless it dies first.

And what you put in the ground is not the plant that will grow, but only a dry little seed of wheat or whatever it is you are planting.

Then God gives it a new body—just the kind he wants it to have. A different kind of plant grows from each kind of seed.

And just as there are different kinds of seeds and plants, so also there are different kinds of flesh—whether of humans, animals, birds, or fish.

There are bodies in the heavens, and there are bodies on earth. The glory of the heavenly bodies is different from the beauty of the earthly bodies.

The sun has one kind of glory, while the moon and stars each have another kind. And even the stars differ from each other in their beauty and brightness.

It is the same way for the resurrection of the dead. Our earthly bodies, which die and decay, will be different when they are resurrected, for they will never die.

Our bodies now disappoint us, but when they are raised, they will be full of glory. They are weak now, but when they are raised, they will be full of power.

They are natural human bodies now, but when they are raised, they will be spiritual bodies. For just as there are natural bodies, so also there are spiritual bodies.

The Scriptures tell us, "The first man, Adam, became a living person." But the last Adam—that is, Christ—is a life-giving Spirit.

What came first was the natural body, then the spiritual body comes later.

Adam, the first man, was made from the dust of the earth, while Christ, the second man, came from heaven.

Every human being has an earthly body just like Adam's, but our heavenly bodies will be just like Christ's.

Just as we are now like Adam, the man of the earth, so we will someday be like Christ, the man from heaven.

What I am saying, dear brothers and sisters, is that flesh and blood cannot inherit the Kingdom of God. These perishable bodies of ours are not able to live forever.

But let me tell you a wonderful secret God has revealed to us. Not all of us will die, but we will all be transformed.

It will happen in a moment, in the blinking of an eye, when the last trumpet is blown. For when the trumpet sounds, the Christians who have died will be raised with transformed bodies. And then we who are living will be transformed so that we will never die.

For our perishable earthly bodies must be transformed into heavenly bodies that will never die. (1 Corinthians 15:35-53 NLT)

All right, folks. In case you didn't realize it, what you were reading is one of the most informative portions of Scripture on the subject of life after death. It tells us in clear, simple terms what's going to become of us when we're quickened.

Paul started off by referring to the question as "foolish," because apparently some people of his day were under the foolish, mistaken impression that they kept their same, human, physical, flesh-and-blood body even after their future resurrection. He immediately corrected that notion:

> When you put a seed into the ground, it doesn't grow into a plant unless it dies first. And what you put in the ground is not the plant that will grow, but only a dry little seed of wheat or whatever it is you are planting. Then God gives it a new body—just the kind he wants it to have. A different kind of plant grows from each kind of seed. (vv. 36-38)

His discussion uses an analogy that even a child can understand, so there's nothing difficult to grasp. He talked about seeds, and what seeds eventually become. Now just think of any seed that pops into your mind. He mentioned a wheat seed, but maybe you're thinking of a pumpkin seed, a sunflower seed, or even a grapefruit seed. The precise variety doesn't matter. None of those seeds resemble the actual produce from which it comes, but they all become something that generally resembles the original produce.

You already know that a pumpkin seed is quite different from a fully grown pumpkin. Same with a sunflower seed and an actual sunflower in full bloom. They're two very different things. And for anyone to mistake a grapefruit seed for a grapefruit is just . . . well . . . fruity. "God gives it a new body—just the kind he wants it to have. A different kind of plant grows from each kind of seed." That's pretty self-explanatory. After each seed dies, it receives a new kind of body when it grows into the pumpkin, for instance. But that brand-new pumpkin, though it's not the exact same plant from which the seed came, looks pretty much the same as the previous pumpkin.

> And just as there are different kinds of seeds and plants, so also there are different kinds of flesh— whether of humans, animals, birds, or fish. There are bodies in the heavens, and there are bodies on earth. The glory of the heavenly bodies is different from the beauty of the earthly bodies. The sun has one kind of glory, while the moon and stars each have another kind. And even the stars differ from each other in their beauty and brightness. (vv. 39-41)

Here we're told some more obvious things, starting with different kinds of flesh. Human beings, cats, birds, and fish are all creatures made up of flesh. But it doesn't take a biology whiz to realize that the bodies of human beings differ greatly from the bodies of purring, paw-footed cats, which differ greatly from our feathered friends flying in the sky, which differ greatly from salmon and guppies in the waters of the world.

And the bodies of all these creations on Earth are all very different from the bodies of items dwelling in the sky, such as the sun, moon, planets, and countless stars. Not only do the heavenly bodies look different, they come in a wide variety of sizes, and they have no muscles, no nervous system, and no blood pumping through any veins. Each different celestial object has its own unique content, appearance, and beauty. Long before there were deep-space telescopes probing the uncharted sections of the universe, Paul pointed out correctly that even the stars differ from each other in their glory. Today, our modern technology has allowed us to catalog many stars based on their differing characteristics, such as brightness, size, chemical composition, etc.

The Bible passage goes on to say:

> It is the same way for the resurrection of the dead. Our earthly bodies, which die and decay, will be

different when they are resurrected, for they will never die. Our bodies now disappoint us, but when they are raised, they will be full of glory. They are weak now, but when they are raised, they will be full of power. They are natural human bodies now, but when they are raised, they will be spiritual bodies. For just as there are natural bodies, so also there are spiritual bodies. (vv. 42-44)

The analogy to human bodies and the future resurrection of the dead gets discussed here with uncanny specificity. The Bible explains what even children know: When we die, our earthly, physical bodies get planted in the ground. Remember, this is still a comparison to seeds, since seeds get planted in the ground to die but eventually become something far greater and glorious than the seed, though looking similar to the original produce.

When our natural, physical, earthly bodies are put into the grave, they're described as being buried in weakness and decay. But that's when the miraculous happens. Just as seeds get transformed into something so much greater than they were when planted in the soil, so our bodies will become something almost inconceivably more fantastic. They'll be raised not only in glory and in strength, but will consist of an entirely different substance—spirit!

Read verse 44 once again and just let your mind absorb what your own Bible is telling you: "They are natural human bodies now, but when they are raised, they will be spiritual bodies. For just as there are natural bodies, so also there are spiritual bodies."

No matter how close to God you are right now, your body is still a natural human, physical body. You've spent your entire life living in your natural body. Through your five senses of seeing, hearing, smelling, tasting, and touching, you know very well what you've experienced. You know what it's like to have pleasurable, physical sensations and what it's like to feel physical pain. But the Bible says our natural human bodies are going to be raised as something else—as spiritual bodies. In other words, bodies made up of spirit. The same stuff God consists of! Remember, we're made in the image and likeness of God, and that's our eventual destiny, to be children of God in the family of God. We'll still resemble our previous selves as far as form and shape, but the ingredients will be different. We're still going to have a head, but it will be a head consisting of spirit. We'll still have a torso, shoulders, arms, hands, legs, and feet. But they won't be made up of flesh and blood any longer. They'll be composed of spirit.

Continuing now, we see:

> The Scriptures tell us, "The first man, Adam, became a living person." But the last Adam- that is, Christ—is a life-giving Spirit. (v. 45)

The King James Version translates the final part of this verse by saying: "The last Adam was made a quickening spirit."

There's that Q-word again. Quickening. And it's making a direct reference to the first person ever made, Adam, who was given a temporary, physical, flesh-and-blood life here on Earth in a natural body. But then it says the last Adam, identified as Jesus Christ, was made a quickening (immortal-life-giving) spirit. Remember, Jesus Christ has already been resurrected and quickened by His Father into His immortal, glorified, spirit-composed body in the God family, where He's seen sometimes sitting and sometimes standing at the right hand of the Father. And as we've read, Jesus also has the power to quicken, or give eternal life to, anyone He wishes.

Now just in case you're still not understanding it, Paul continued his explanation about the big change we experience from one body type to another:

> What came first was the natural body, then the spiritual body comes later. Adam, the first man, was made from the dust of the earth, while Christ, the second man, came from heaven. Every human being has an earthly body just like Adam's, but our heavenly bodies will be just like Christ's. Just as we are now like Adam, the man of the earth, so we will someday be like Christ, the man from heaven. (vv. 46-49)

These verses are so simple and direct, it's really difficult to misunderstand them. They mean exactly what they say. As we live our regular, physical lives here—whether it's eating, drinking, breathing, belching, perspiring, going to the bathroom, sleeping, or waking up in the morning— we do so in a natural, flesh-and-blood, physical body. But Paul said the spiritual body—the body composed of spirit—"comes later," as in after we're resurrected from the dead. It hasn't happened yet to anyone with the sole exception of Jesus.

Paul said that Adam had been made from the ground, the dust of the earth, but Jesus, who came from the invisible, spirit dimension of heaven, is now made up of what the God family in heaven consists of, and that, of course, is spirit. You and I are now like Adam, the earthly man, because we're made up of the same stuff Adam was. But Scripture directly declares that someday in the future, OUR HEAVENLY BODIES WILL BE JUST LIKE CHRIST'S! We'll be comprised of the same exact material. "We will someday be like Christ"!

Paul continued:

> What I am saying, dear brothers and sisters, is that our physical bodies cannot inherit the Kingdom of God. (v. 50)

Other versions, including the KJV, NKJV, and NIV, all render this as "flesh and blood cannot inherit the kingdom of God."

It's what I mentioned earlier and is key to understanding and grasping the mysteries of the kingdom of God. Our flesh-and-blood, physical bodies simply can't be in the kingdom of God. It's impossible. They'll simply not exist as they do now. They'll first have to undergo the change, the quickening. They'll be transformed into their immortal, spirit-composed bodies that all members of the God family will be granted. It may seem surreal to you, but it's on the pages of the Bible and has been there for centuries.

Second Coming Attraction

Let's wrap up Paul's thoughts on the matter. In verse 51, he stated: "But let me tell you a wonderful secret God has revealed to us."

There's that word again—"secret." It's a wonderful secret, indeed, but it's being explained in clear terms now so everyone can understand God's tremendous plan:

> Not all of us will die, but we will all be transformed. It will happen in a moment, in the blinking of an eye, when the last trumpet is blown. For when the trumpet sounds, the Christians who have died will be raised with transformed bodies. And then we who are living will be transformed so that we will never die. For our perishable earthly bodies must be transformed into heavenly bodies that will never die. (vv. 51-53)

These last three verses are just bursting with incredible information about the quickening—the moment our physical, mortal bodies are transformed into immortal ones.

They indicate the procedure is a very fast one, taking place "in a moment, in the blinking of an eye," or what we might call a split second. It's going to be virtually instantaneous, much more rapid than a seed sprouting into some kind of fruit or vegetable.

We're told that "the Christians who have died will be raised with transformed bodies." That's straightforward, and should no longer be a surprise to anyone. Deceased believers will suddenly have life injected into them, but this time it will be eternal life, so they're then able to live forever in their newly transformed, non-perishable bodies.

But there's another intriguing part of this wonderful secret. It says that "not all of us will die." In other words, there will be some believers who will not be dead in the grave when they're quickened into their new bodies of spirit. There will be Christian people in the future still walking around on terra firma when suddenly, in a virtual instant, their physical bodies will be transformed into their glorious, spirit bodies.

And when does this occur? When we let the Bible speak for itself, it's clear the momentous event takes place at the Second Coming of Jesus. Only a few verses earlier in this same chapter of 1 Corinthians, Paul noted:

> Just as everyone dies because we all belong to Adam, everyone who belongs to Christ will be given new life. But there is an order to this resurrection: Christ was raised as the first of the harvest; then all who belong to Christ will be raised when he comes back. (vv. 22-23 NLT)

This is very plain. Christ has already been raised back to His immortal life, and it's when He returns to Earth, and not one moment before, that His followers receive the same reward.

We've also seen some simple, straightforward comments about this from Peter:

> And I, too, will share his glory and his honor WHEN HE RETURNS. (1 Peter 5:1 NLT, emphasis added)

> ...and WHEN THE CHIEF SHEPHERD APPEARS, you will receive the crown of glory that does not fade away. (1 Peter 5:4 NKJV, emphasis added)

To confirm this time frame, Paul also explained that the change takes place "when the last trumpet is blown. For when the trumpet sounds, the Christians who have died will be raised with transformed bodies. And then we who are living will be transformed so that we will never die."

Here's something new to consider. There's a trumpet that'll be blown when all believers (both living and dead) are quickened, and it's referred to as "the last trumpet." But what's all this about? Do people need to learn to play the trumpet? And when is it supposed to be blown?

Once again, there's no need for guesswork, because Scripture itself provides the answers. The blasting of the last trumpet is mentioned in several New Testament books, all having to do with the moment when Jesus Christ is descending out of His unseen dwelling place in heaven and making His triumphant return to Planet Earth. Call it a Second Coming attraction.

In the gospel of Matthew, we read about some of God's end-time actions: "He will use a loud trumpet to send his angels all around the earth, and they will gather his chosen people from every part of the world." (24:31 NCV)

The loud trumpet sounding at the time of the quickening will originate in heaven, and will be heard as people on Earth are looking up into the sky and realize that everything they've ever been told about the return of Jesus to Earth is actually true, whether they believed it or not. Verse 31 comes on the heels of two other verses providing more details:

> Immediately after the tribulation of those days the sun will be darkened, and the moon will not give its light; the stars will fall from heaven, and the powers of the heavens will be shaken. Then the sign of the Son of Man will appear in heaven, and then all the tribes of the earth will mourn, and they will see the Son of Man coming on the clouds of heaven with power and great glory. And He will send His angels with a great sound of a trumpet, and they will gather together His elect from the four winds, from one end of heaven to the other. (vv. 29-31, NKJV)

The great quickening is slated to follow many other events that still have not taken place. These verses mention tribulation, a time of never-before-seen trouble for human beings. It also talks about eye-catching sights in the sky, from the sun and moon suddenly becoming dark to our eyes, to stars falling. Other parts of the Bible say "the stars will stop shining." (Joel 3:15, NCV) As everyone is gazing upward to see what's next, they'll finally view the Creator of the universe, known by a variety of names, including the King of kings, the Word, and Jesus Christ, descending in the atmosphere to make His long-promised return. While faithful Christians will be thrilled, most people will not be happy about this at all. In fact, the Bible says "all the tribes of the earth will mourn."

Now, you might be wondering why most inhabitants of this world will be mourning. The simple fact of the matter is that most people are not true followers of Jesus, and most would prefer their own evil way of life to continue.

Jesus noted that "the Light has come into the world, but they did not want light. They wanted darkness, because they were doing evil things. All who do evil hate the light and will not come to the light, because it will show all the evil things they do." (John 3:19-20 NCV)

Most people just don't want to be told what to do, and be informed, even if it's by someone trying to help, that the way they've been living their life is wrong. Of course, atheists and believers of other faiths will likely be pooping their pants the moment Jesus comes back because they'll finally realize that everything on which they had based their lives has been completely false and that the God of the Bible is the real deal.

The series of events surrounding Jesus' descent through the atmosphere is described by Paul in another letter he wrote, and there's nothing complex about it:

> What we tell you now is the Lord's own message. We who are living when the Lord comes again will not go before those who have already died. The Lord himself will come down from heaven with a loud command, with the voice of the archangel, and with the trumpet call of God. And those who have died believing in Christ will rise first. After that, we who are still alive will be gathered up with them in the clouds to meet the Lord in the air. (1 Thessalonians 4:15-17 NCV)

In this account, we see exactly what we've read before in other places. The Lord Jesus is coming out of His unseen dwelling place with "the trumpet call of God." This will apparently be an audible blast of a trumpet that possibly can be heard worldwide. Paul again talked about the timetable of those being quickened into their immortal spirit bodies.

He specifically noted that "We who are living when the Lord comes again will not go before those who have already died. . . . And those who have died believing in Christ will rise first."

It couldn't be any clearer. All dead persons who have been true believers in Jesus—whether it was Noah or Moses back in the Old Testament days, or Peter or Paul in the first century, or you yourself if you've made the decision to live your life according to God's instructions and have passed away by the time Jesus comes back—will be the first ones to rise. They'll be quickened to their immortal, spirit bodies just ahead of any Christians who happen to be alive on the day of Christ's return.

And Paul noted, "After that, we who are still alive will be gathered up with them in the clouds to meet the Lord in the air."

This is not rocket science, folks. We're just reading the words on the page. They inform us that immediately after the dead Christians wake up from their mortal slumber, whether it was five minutes or five thousand years in the grave, all other believers who are still alive while they watch Jesus slowly float down toward Earth will be quickened and gathered up in the air to meet Jesus as He continues His descent.

The book of Revelation is yet another place that provides an in-depth description of events surrounding the return of Jesus, and it too mentions this blasting of trumpets. In fact, it talks about seven angels sounding their trumpets in numerical order:

> And I saw the seven angels who stand before God,
> and they were given seven trumpets. . . . Then the
> seven angels with the seven trumpets prepared to
> blow their mighty blasts. (Revelation 8:2,6 NLT)

An onslaught of horrific events is predicted for the time immediately preceding the return of Jesus, as each of these angels sound their respective trumpets. For instance, when the first trumpet is blown, we're told "a third of the trees were burned up, and all green grass was burned up." (v. 7 NKJV)

> Then the second angel sounded: And something like a great mountain burning with fire was thrown into the sea, and a third of the sea became blood. And a third of the living creatures in the sea died, and a third of the ships were destroyed. (vv. 8-9 NKJV)

This sounds like it could be a giant meteor smashing into the ocean and wreaking all kinds of havoc, but whatever it is, Scripture makes clear that a whopping one-third of everything that lives in the water will be killed, not to mention one-third of all ships being done for.

You can read the entire eighth chapter of Revelation and beyond for more of the gory details, but I'm focusing here on the infinitely more positive, amazing future that's foretold for you and me once all the nastiness is finished.

The "last trumpet" we originally read about in 1 Corinthians 15:52 is alluded to in the tenth chapter of Revelation in stunning fashion: "In the days when the seventh angel is ready to blow his trumpet, God's secret will be finished. This secret is the Good News God told to his servants, the prophets." (v. 7 NCV)

Wow! Once again, in the final book of the Bible, Scripture itself talks about "God's secret." Not only that, it says the secret will be finished, as in the wondrous plan finally being accomplished and fulfilled. The secret is the very Good News that God throughout thousands of years told to the people He was working with—His prophets—but kept hidden from countless others on purpose. The divine secret is the Good News of the magnificent, eternal purpose of the God family finally coming to fruition in all its glory. The kingdom of God will be a reality as it arrives on planet Earth:

> Then the seventh angel sounded: And there were loud voices in heaven, saying, "The kingdoms of this world have become the kingdoms of our Lord and of His Christ, and He shall reign forever and ever!" (Revelation 11:15 NKJV)

When the last trumpet from the seventh angel blows, Jesus Christ will personally replace all the other governments on the planet. His dead followers will be quickened into their immortal, spirit-composed bodies as they rise out of their graves. They'll ascend into the sky as Jesus is descending. Almost immediately after they're raised from the dead, all the other believers who still happen to be alive at the time will be transformed in a millisecond into their eternally alive bodies, having undergone their own quickening, and they too will be gathered from points all over the Earth by angels to meet Jesus in the air as He continues His descent.

To my knowledge, no major motion picture has ever depicted this extraordinary event, and I seriously doubt Hollywood has the gonads to produce one. But you don't need Hollywood to portray it to understand it. The Bible itself gives you plenty of details to picture the heretofore greatest news event of all time: the return of the King and the birth of all His true followers into their brand new, glorified, spirit-composed, immortal bodies as consummate members of the family of God!

Shine Like the Son

Once people are born into the divine family and are glorified as sons and daughters of God, there are certain characteristics they'll have in connection with their newly transformed bodies. Among them is the fact that God's children will be completely sinless. That's correct. It will be impossible to sin any longer:

"Whoever has been born of God does not sin, for
His seed remains in him; and he cannot sin, because
he has been born of God." (1 John 3:9 NKJV)

Many people hear that word "sin," and they're not quite sure
what it means. Some may suggest it's drinking alcohol, gambling,
or staying out late at night. But the Bible actually defines what sin
is. Just five verses before what we've just read, Scripture says in 1
John 3:4 that "sin is lawlessness" (NKJV). The King James Version
says "sin is the transgression of the law," as in the breaking of God's
law, which is summed up in the famous Ten Commandments.
When people violate an instruction from God, that is sin.

But once the jump is made from physical bodies to spiritual
ones, being literally "born OF GOD," born into the actual family
of God, the Bible indicates sin will not be possible, because God's
newly born children simply "cannot sin." They'll be unable to
break God's law. Those in God's own family will be in complete
harmony with the eternal laws of God, so that they can't even
violate one of the instructions unintentionally.

But that's just the beginning. There's much more in store,
including a certain brightness that will actually shine from them.
Yes, the children of God will be sparkling with a glamorous
splendor they don't possess at present in these earthly, physical
bodies. But once the big change occurs, look out.

As we previously read in 1 John 3:2 regarding the children of
God, "it has not yet been revealed what we shall be, but we know that
when He is revealed, we shall be like Him . . . " (1 John 3:2 NKJV)

We've also seen:

By his power to rule all things, he will change
our humble bodies and make them like his own
glorious body. (Philippians 3:21 NCV)

And:

> . . . our heavenly bodies will be just like Christ's.
> (1 Corinthians 15:48 NLT)

The Bible plainly says our bodies are going to be like Jesus' body once He returns and quickens His followers. And as we've also discovered, Jesus in His current glorified state is a brightly shining spirit being: "His head and hair were white like wool, as white as snow, and his eyes were like flames of fire. His feet were like bronze that glows hot in a furnace, and his voice was like the noise of flooding water. . . . He looked like the sun shining at its brightest time." (Revelation 1:14-16 NCV)

To say He's a dazzling sight is an understatement. The Creator is said to be shining like the sun when it's at its brightest time. He doesn't have dark-colored hair. It's as white as snow, as white as wool. His eyes are blazingly bright as if they were flames of fire, and His feet are said to be glowing like hot bronze that's melted in a furnace. He's obviously emitting light from top to bottom.

We're given glimpses of His radiant body and hands in the Old Testament, where the prophet Habakkuk noted, "He is like a bright light. Rays of light shine from his hand, and there he hides his power." (Habakkuk 3:4 NCV)

Another account of Jesus' glory is found in the book of Ezekiel, when that prophet was allowed to see what the Creator looked like before leaving heaven to come live among human beings: "From his waist up, he looked like gleaming amber, flickering like a fire. And from his waist down, he looked like a burning flame, shining with splendor. All around him was a glowing halo, like a rainbow shining through the clouds. This was the way the glory of the LORD appeared to me." (Ezekiel 1:27-28 NLT)

Once again, we're given an array of descriptors including "gleaming amber," "flickering in a fire," "burning flame," "shining with splendor," "glowing," and "rainbow shining." In other words, there's a polished, fiery brilliance emanating from and surrounding Jesus. He's so bright, in fact, that typical sunshine won't be needed in the Jerusalem of the future when He takes up residence there: "The city had no need of the sun or of the moon to shine in it, for the glory of God illuminated it. The Lamb is its light." (Revelation 21:23 NKJV)

But don't forget, faithful believers also will eventually be like Jesus. Not only will they see Him as He is in all His candescent splendor, they too will shine with the brilliance of celestial objects.

The promise about shining bodies was first made in the Old Testament, where we read:

> Many of those whose bodies lie dead and buried will rise up, some to everlasting life and some to shame and everlasting disgrace. Those who are wise will SHINE AS BRIGHT AS THE SKY, and those who lead many to righteousness will SHINE LIKE THE STARS forever. (Daniel 12:2-3 NLT, emphasis added)

In the New Testament, Jesus personally repeated the promise of shining bodies for righteous believers:

> The Son of Man will send out His angels, and they will gather out of His kingdom all things that offend, and those who practice lawlessness, and will cast them into the furnace of fire. There will be wailing and gnashing of teeth. Then the righteous will shine forth as the sun in the kingdom of their Father. He who has ears to hear, let him hear! (Matthew 13:41-43, NKJV)

Did you catch that? Once Jesus returns and his angels clear out the wicked elements, presumably such as Satan the devil, He said the righteous (those who are obedient to God) will SHINE FORTH AS THE SUN IN THE KINGDOM OF THEIR FATHER. This hasn't taken place yet because the kingdom of God has not yet been brought to Earth. No one is shining like the sun here right now. But they will be glowing in the days ahead once they're quickened into their immortal, spirit bodies upon the return of Jesus.

While Jesus was speaking about events in the future, there are a few historical instances in the Bible that actually foreshadow the shine to come. Yes, it's ironic to use the term "foreshadow" when it comes to describing something that shines, but hey, that's the way it is.

All the way back in the second book of the Old Testament, when Moses had just received the famous Ten Commandments from God on two tablets of stone, the Bible says the face of Moses began to glow with brightness. Beams of light were actually shooting out from his face! Here's the account:

> When Moses came down from Mount Sinai with the two tablets of the covenant law in his hands, he was not aware that his face was radiant because he had spoken with the LORD. When Aaron and all the Israelites saw Moses, his face was radiant, and they were afraid to come near him. But Moses called to them; so Aaron and all the leaders of the community came back to him, and he spoke to them. Afterward all the Israelites came near him, and he gave them all the commands the LORD had given him on Mount Sinai. When Moses finished speaking to them, he put a veil over his face. But whenever he entered the LORD's presence to speak with him, he removed the veil until he came out. And when he came out and told the Israelites what

he had been commanded, they saw that his face was radiant. Then Moses would put the veil back over his face until he went in to speak with the LORD. (Exodus 34:29-35 NIV)

This is nothing short of a miraculous occurrence, and few people seem to talk or write about it today. The face of Moses was shining so brightly, it freaked out his fellow Israelites, and he ended up putting a veil over his head to hide the radiance. He would remove the covering only to talk with God face to face, and then put it back on when in the presence of his fellow countrymen. The reason this is in the Bible, folks, is because it's giving you a small hint, a fractional preview, of what's in store for us when we're quickened into the family of God. We'll be shining with light!

Other appearances of brilliance are briefly mentioned in the New Testament. In the book of Acts, we're told the story of Stephen, one of the first Christian champions, who performed great signs and wonders before he was arrested on false charges and put on trial for his life. During his prosecution, a bright glow suddenly enveloped his face:

At this point everyone in the council stared at Stephen, because his face became as bright as an angel's. (Acts 6:15 NLT)

Another illuminating preview of the kingdom involved Jesus Himself in an incident often called "the Transfiguration." It's a long word, but it simply refers to Jesus' whole appearance changing during a supernatural vision given to some of his apostles. Scripture states: "Six days later, Jesus took Peter, James, and John, the brother of James, up on a high mountain by themselves. While they watched, Jesus' appearance was changed; his face became bright like the sun, and his clothes became white as light." (Matthew 17:1-2 NCV)

Once again, this was just a temporary display of whiteness and brightness, but it's a preview of what's in store for all those who make it into the kingdom, because then "the righteous will shine forth as the sun in the kingdom of their Father." (Matthew 13:43 NKJV)

Divine Dining

I hope by now the sensational truth of what we're intended to become in the future is really sinking in. We're not going to be flesh-and-blood human beings in the coming kingdom. We're going to be divine members of God's very own family, known as the children of God.

Now the thought may have crossed your mind: *Will we be eating food and drinking beverages once our bodies have been transformed from physical to spirit?* This is an interesting question because as spirit beings with eternal life infused into us, there will be no chance of dying again—none whatsoever. That's what Jesus promised: "And they will never die again. . . . They are children of God raised up to new life." (Luke 20:36 NLT)

In our current physical form as mortal people in this life, we already know that we need to shovel some nutrition down our pie-hole on a regular basis. It's no secret that if we completely stop eating food and drinking water, we'll eventually drop dead. But in our new future state, having literally been born again into our spirit bodies, it will simply be impossible to die again, so ingesting food and water to sustain life will be irrelevant. Being immortal means we'll have no need of food in order to stay alive.

Having said that, if you're a person who really enjoys certain food and drink, you've got reason to rejoice, because you won't have to give them up. There's plenty of biblical evidence to indicate we'll be enjoying food and beverages in the coming kingdom in our transformed bodies.

But before looking ahead to the feasting of the future, it's important to take note of one of the most underreported dining events of the ancient past, way back in the very first book of the Bible. It reveals how the Creator of the universe, Jesus Christ, along with two angels who were all temporarily appearing as men, actually sat down and enjoyed a meal of meat, bread, cheese, and milk with Abraham.

I really don't know why this incident is so rarely talked about, but in just eight verses, it's remarkably educational about the inhabitants of the spirit world, whether they're members of the God kingdom or the angelic kingdom. Here's the account, uninterrupted for your reading pleasure:

> The LORD appeared again to Abraham while he was camped near the oak grove belonging to Mamre. One day about noon, as Abraham was sitting at the entrance to his tent, he suddenly noticed three men standing nearby. He got up and ran to meet them, welcoming them by bowing low to the ground.
>
> "My lord," he said, "if it pleases you, stop here for a while. Rest in the shade of this tree while my servants get some water to wash your feet. Let me prepare some food to refresh you. Please stay awhile before continuing on your journey."
>
> "All right," they said. "Do as you have said."
>
> So Abraham ran back to the tent and said to Sarah, "Quick! Get three measures of your best flour, and bake some bread."
>
> Then Abraham ran out to the herd and chose a fat calf and told a servant to hurry and butcher it. When the food was ready, he took some cheese

curds and milk and the roasted meat, and he served it to the men. As they ate, Abraham waited on them there beneath the trees. (Genesis 18:1-8, NLT)

All right, the first thing to notice is that those who dwell in the spirit world, including the Lord Himself, have the ability to appear as human beings—in this instance, men! Remember, this is near the very beginning of the Bible, thousands of years before Jesus was born as a human through Mary.

It's not God the Father making the appearance, because later in the New Testament, Jesus personally said more than once that no man has ever seen the Father:

And the Father himself who sent me has given proof about me. You have never heard his voice or seen what he looks like. (John 5:37 NCV)

Not that anyone has ever seen the Father; only I, who was sent from God, have seen him. (John 6:46 NLT)

Plus, in the gospel of John, Jesus actually made reference to this lunch meeting He had with Abraham many centuries before: "Your father Abraham rejoiced to see my day: and he saw it, and was glad." (8:56 KJV)

So here in the book of Genesis, we have Jesus Himself in one of His pre-human-birth appearances getting invited to a meal by His friend Abraham. Jesus and His companions were standing outside, and Abraham offered to wash the trio's feet before they ate. Yes, they have feet. Remember, we've already read that God looks like human beings, and human beings look like God, because people were created in the image and likeness of God. Jesus and the angels agreed to stay, eat, and even have their feet washed: "All right," they said. "Do as you have said."

But the story gets even more fascinating because typical, physical food—the kind of food that you and I consume today—was prepared for these spirit beings to eat! Abraham instructed his wife to grab some of their best flour to bake some bread. He then ran out to his own herd of animals to choose a fat calf to be butchered in a hurry by one of his workers. It took some time to get everything prepared, just as any meal today takes some time, but once the food was ready, Jesus and the two angels who were all appearing as men actually ate roasted meat and cheese curds, and they guzzled down some milk!

I don't want you to skip over this without realizing the significance of the lunch with Abraham, because it seems no one in church ever talks about it. We're told that the Lord God Himself, the Creator of the universe who is an eternal spirit being, ate regular, physical, material food—meat, cheese, and milk—the very same physical items that we human beings eat today in our physical, material, mortal, flesh-and-blood bodies. It's really enthralling to consider.

Once this food entered their mouths and was swallowed, where did it go? Was it digested the way human beings digest food? Did God and these angelic men have internal organs producing hydrochloric acid to break up the proteins and fats? Was there any waste product formed through an excretory system? Or did it just vanish into nothingness? Unfortunately, the Bible never answers these intriguing questions. But all foods, with their wide variety of delicious flavors, are divine creations of the divine God, so it makes sense that they would be desired and consumed by their Maker. The main point I'm conveying is that even from the earliest book of the Bible, we're shown that spirit beings can and do eat regular food for enjoyment, even if they don't need it to exist.

Moving ahead to the New Testament, we see the same situation holding true for Jesus after He was killed and resurrected. During a brief appearance in front of His apostles, Jesus is shown to have eaten some fish:

> While they still could not believe it because they were amazed and happy, Jesus said to them, "Do you have any food here?" They gave him a piece of broiled fish. While the followers watched, Jesus took the fish and ate it. (Luke 24:41-43 NCV)

During a brief speech, Peter also noted that Jesus both ate and drank with the disciples after His resurrection: "And we are those witnesses who ate and drank with him after he was raised from the dead." (Acts 10:41 NCV)

Jesus Himself mentioned that He'd eventually dine with believers: "Here I am! I stand at the door and knock. If anyone hears my voice and opens the door, I will come in and eat with him, and he with me." (Revelation 3:20 NIV)

And looking ahead to the distant future when the kingdom of God is in full swing and believers have been changed to spirit, Jesus said both He and his followers would be eating and drinking together at the same table: "Just as my Father has given me a kingdom, I also give you a kingdom so you may eat and drink at my table in my kingdom." (Luke 22:29-30 NCV)

Are you getting this? We're going to be seated at the very table of God in the coming kingdom of God, and we'll be eating and drinking with the Creator of the universe!

Even though Jesus said He'd be dining with his fellow brothers and sisters once they've been changed to their immortal status, He mentioned some items He'd avoid until He personally returns to usher in the kingdom.

For instance, just before Jesus was executed, He mentioned at the famous Last Supper that this particular Passover meal of lamb and bitter herbs was going to be His last Passover meal for a long time:

> He said to them, "I wanted very much to eat this Passover meal with you before I suffer. I will not eat another Passover meal until it is given its true meaning in the kingdom of God." (Luke 22:15-16 NCV)

Not only was he referring to the actual food items on the menu, but apparently the wine as well, as He added: "I will not drink again from the fruit of the vine until God's kingdom comes." (Luke 22:18 NCV)

Again, it's not a permanent abstention from these food items. It's just until Jesus appears out of the unseen dimension of heaven and comes back to administer the kingdom of God here on Earth. But it clearly says Jesus will again be eating in the future after His return.

In fact, an Old Testament prophecy concerning the Second Coming of Jesus actually mentions a grand food event, a famous feast that will take place with Christ once He has returned.

> And it shall come to pass that everyone who is left of all the nations which came against Jerusalem shall go up from year to year to worship the King, the LORD of hosts, and to keep the Feast of Tabernacles. (Zechariah 14:16 NKJV)

For those not familiar with this feast, it's actually a weeklong, food-filled celebration commanded by God: "You shall observe the Feast of Tabernacles seven days, when you have gathered from your threshing floor and from your winepress. And you shall rejoice in your feast, you and your son and your daughter, your male servant and your female servant and the Levite, the stranger and the fatherless and the widow, who are within your gates. Seven days you shall keep a sacred feast to the LORD your God in the place which the LORD chooses, because the LORD your God will bless you in all your produce and in all the work of your hands, so that you surely rejoice." (Deuteronomy 16:13-15 NKJV)

In that vein of celebration meals, the book of Revelation mentions a wedding meal involving Jesus, who is often referred to as the Lamb of God: "Blessed are those who have been invited to the wedding meal of the Lamb!" (Revelation 19:9 NCV)

Revelation also talks about a few more mysterious food items for those who have been changed into spirit beings. One is referred to as hidden manna: "Everyone who is victorious will eat of the manna that has been hidden away in heaven." (Revelation 2:17 NLT)

The New Testament provides no other revelatory details about hidden manna secreted away in the unseen dimension of God's dwelling place. But manna is discussed numerous times in the Old Testament, as a mysterious food substance that sustained the Israelites during their forty years in the wilderness.

The word "manna" literally means "What is it?" because the Israelites had no clue what it actually was, and even to this day, no one is certain of manna's precise composition. If you think about it, it sounds a bit funny. People might say, "I had a big bowl of 'What is it?' for breakfast." But Scripture does give a few more clues about its texture and taste, explaining, "It was like white coriander seed, and the taste of it was like wafers made with honey." (Exodus 16:31 NKJV)

The other mystery food mentioned in the final book of the Bible comes from the tree of life. Yes, the same tree of life that's talked about at the very start of Genesis in the famous garden of Eden.

Adam and Eve were given the chance to eat from it to gain eternal life; however, they chose to eat the forbidden fruit of another tree, the tree of knowledge of good and evil. (Genesis 3:6)

But one of the final promises Jesus is ever recorded as making is that the quickened children of God will actually be eating produce from the tree of life:

> To him who overcomes I will give to eat from the tree of life, which is in the midst of the Paradise of God. (Revelation 2:7 NKJV)

A little more information about the tree's whereabouts and its produce is provided later in the book, as we're told:

> In the middle of its street, and on either side of the river, was the tree of life, which bore twelve fruits, each tree yielding its fruit every month. The leaves of the tree were for the healing of the nations. (Revelation 22:2 NKJV)

According to the Bible, the tree of life is not some figurative metaphor. It's an actual tree that grows from the ground near a river in the paradise of God, and produces twelve fruits, one for each month of the year. All those transformed into their immortal spirit bodies will be granted the right and ability to eat from that tree. The tree of life was intended for the original human beings to eat from before they chose to disobey God, but its produce is going to be offered to those who overcome and are granted eternal life. So there's absolutely no doubt that the immortal, spirit-composed children of God will be eating in the kingdom of God.

Knowledge Is Power

If we're born into the family of God, it also means we're going to have some brand new abilities that we currently don't possess. The first difference we might realize immediately is an infusion of knowledge and wisdom, a whole lot of information and understanding that our puny, finite minds just can't handle at this time. We might think we know a lot right now, but we really understand only a small fraction of all the knowledge in the visible universe, not to mention the unseen one in the spirit world.

Paul likened our current level of understanding to looking through a dark piece of glass or at a poor mirror, but added that everything will be made crystal clear once we're in the kingdom: "Now we see things imperfectly as in a poor mirror, but then we will see everything with perfect clarity. All that I know now is partial and incomplete, but then I will know everything completely, just as God knows me now." (1 Corinthians 13:12 NLT)

If there is any being that knows everything there is to know, it's the Creator of all things, and the Bible itself makes that clear, explaining "the LORD is the God of knowledge" (1 Samuel 2:3 NKJV). The New Century Version translates that as "The Lord is a God who knows everything."

It's not just material knowledge, but also the thoughts inside everyone's minds, "for He knows the secrets of the heart." (Psalm 44:21 NKJV)

And Paul praised the extent of God's wisdom and knowledge, saying, "Oh, the depth of the riches both of the wisdom and knowledge of God! How unsearchable are His judgments and His ways past finding out!" (Romans 11:33 NKJV) Yes, we simply cannot grasp everything at this time with our finite, physical minds, but remember, we're going to be born into powerful new spirit bodies to be like Jesus. Thus, we can expect a significant boost in knowledge and wisdom so that "we will see everything with perfect clarity," just as Paul said.

Now You See Me, Now You Don't

In addition to knowing a lot more, resurrected believers will also be able to control their own visibility. This ability to be seen or not seen by others has already been demonstrated through the actions of God and the angels. They're all supernatural beings, because their existence and properties are above, or are not subject to, the physical laws of the universe. They can be invisible to our eyes whenever they wish. Unfortunately for us right now, that's most of the time, as many people would love to get a glimpse into the unseen world. But Scripture, in both the Old and New Testaments, tells us of many instances where both God and angels become visible to human beings.

We just read a few moments ago about how Jesus and two angels materialized out of their invisible home of heaven to personally appear to Abraham. In the book of Genesis, they sat down, conversed, and enjoyed a meal with him.

Later, while speaking of Moses, Jesus said He talked with the prophet in person and visibly: "I speak with him face to face, Even plainly, and not in dark sayings; And he sees the form of the LORD." (Numbers 12:8 NKJV)

I realize that many people are simply unaware of such evocative Bible verses, so I'm highlighting them because they're so telling about the nature of God and the spirit world, which is the nature of what we're going to become as part of God's family. Jesus, before He was born as a human being through Mary, would actually materialize in person and have direct discussions with Moses, where Moses could actually see the form and shape of the eternal Creator, a supernatural being composed of spirit.

And it's not just God who has this ability to appear at will. Angels can also leave their invisible realm and show up at any given location. Perhaps the most famous example in the entire Bible is the appearance of an angel—many angels, as a matter of fact—to shepherds who were watching their flocks in the fields outside of Bethlehem. A spirit being told the shepherds to go into town to see for themselves that their Savior Jesus had just been born as a typical human baby:

> And behold, an angel of the Lord stood before them, and the glory of the Lord shone around them, and they were greatly afraid. Then the angel said to them, "Do not be afraid, for behold, I bring you good tidings of great joy which will be to all people. For there is born to you this day in the city of David a Savior, who is Christ the Lord. And this will be the sign to you: You will find a Babe wrapped in swaddling cloths, lying in a manger." And suddenly there was with the angel a multitude of the heavenly host praising God and saying: "Glory to God in the highest, And on earth peace, goodwill toward men!" (Luke 2:9-14 NKJV)

Another well-known manifestation of a spirit took place just after Jesus rose from the dead. An angel left the unseen dimension and made himself visible to the followers of Jesus, as well as some Roman guards who were left trembling upon seeing the spirit:

> An angel of the Lord came down from heaven, went to the tomb, and rolled the stone away from the entrance. Then he sat on the stone. He was shining as bright as lightning, and his clothes were white as snow. The soldiers guarding the tomb shook with fear because of the angel, and they became like dead men. The angel said to the women, "Don't be afraid. I know that you are looking for Jesus, who

has been crucified. He is not here. He has risen from the dead as he said he would. Come and see the place where his body was. (Matthew 28:2-6 NCV)

And we're given a few more details in another gospel about what this angel looked like:

The women entered the tomb and saw a young man wearing a white robe and sitting on the right side, and they were afraid. But the man said, "Don't be afraid. You are looking for Jesus from Nazareth, who has been crucified. He has risen from the dead; he is not here. Look, here is the place they laid him. (Mark 16:5-6 NCV)

In this case, we're told that the angel was appearing in the form of "a young man wearing a white robe."

The appearance of angels in our physical world is not always for some grand, spectacular occasion. In fact, most such instances are the opposite of the magnificent ones that took place with the shepherds of Bethlehem or the discovery of Jesus' empty tomb. They could be everyday, mundane encounters with characters presumed to be people, but are, in reality, spirits appearing out of the unseen world.

The New Testament tells us: "Remember to welcome strangers, because some who have done this have welcomed angels without knowing it." (Hebrews 13:2 NCV)

This single sentence in the Bible is extremely telling about the nature and abilities of spirit beings. It informs us that angels can appear exactly like ordinary, physical human beings. I say this because sometimes when people hear the word "angel," they think of some movie or TV show that portrays angels with giant wings and a human face. While the Bible does indicate that some angels have wings, and even faces of animals, these spirit beings can look like typical human beings whenever they wish, doing the things that humans do. The quote from Hebrews is instructing us to treat everyone with courtesy, respect, and hospitality because it's very possible the person being entertained is not a physical human being, but a spirit inhabitant of the heavenly realm, and specifically an angel!

Now, remember the discussion that Jesus had with Nicodemus. Jesus told the Pharisee, "The wind blows where it wishes, and you hear the sound of it, but cannot tell where it comes from and where it goes. So is everyone who is born of the Spirit." (John 3:8 NKJV)

Jesus was using the analogy of wind to explain what it's like for people once they are born into their spirit bodies. In fact, both the Hebrew and Greek words for "spirit" actually mean "wind," and this is how the ancients heard the word. People become something akin to the wind, in that the wind is invisible and can move in any direction—not just north, south, east, and west. It can go directly up or down, move at any angle, or even spin like a cyclone. These are some of the attributes we're destined to obtain once we're quickened into the family of God. We'll be invisible to the human eye and can travel wherever we like, even though human beings won't be able to tell where we're coming from or where we're going.

Suppose for a moment that Jesus happened to materialize in front of your face right now. You'd really have no specific clue where He came from, except that He was previously somewhere in the unseen realm of heaven. Did He enter via the front door or the back window? Did He walk through a bedroom wall or pass through the roof or the floor? The questions are really irrelevant because the God family, being composed of spirit, transcends the physical laws we understand.

This is precisely how it'll be for us once we're born into our newly transformed, immortal bodies. We'll be able to go wherever we wish, possibly as fast as we like—maybe even at the speed of thought—because we'll be made of spirit and won't have to put up with slow modes of transportation such as physical legs and feet, or planes, trains, and automobiles. If we think ourselves there, we can be there in an instant. Remember, we'll be powerful children of God in the God family.

Matter of Fact

Besides divine knowledge, invisibility, and the power to appear as a human, what else is on the horizon for us when we're composed of spirit? How about the ability to alter physical matter? Indeed, we're intended to have the amazing ability to perform feats we might now call miraculous or supernatural.

There's nothing inherently dark or spooky about something that is supernatural. In fact, it's actually quite uplifting. Something that is supernatural literally means "above the natural," as in above the laws of nature, the physical laws such as gravity or inertia with which we're all familiar. There are many miracles recorded in Scripture, and they're all supernatural occurrences, because they transcend material laws. Some include the famous examples of Jesus changing water into wine at a wedding, and His multiplying a few loaves of bread and a small amount of fish to feed thousands of hungry people. In the case of the water into wine, the gospel account explains:

> In that place there were six stone water jars that the Jews used in their washing ceremony. Each jar held about twenty or thirty gallons.

> Jesus said to the servants, "Fill the jars with water." So they filled the jars to the top.

> Then he said to them, "Now take some out and give it to the master of the feast."
>
> So they took the water to the master. When he tasted it, the water had become wine. He did not know where the wine came from, but the servants who had brought the water knew. The master of the wedding called the bridegroom and said to him, "People always serve the best wine first. Later, after the guests have been drinking awhile, they serve the cheaper wine. But you have saved the best wine till now." (John 2:6-10 NCV)

We're not told if the molecular structure of the water was tweaked so it could change into wine, or if the water itself had been completely replaced by the wine supernaturally. All that we're told is that the stone jars were filled with water, and the liquid became wine, obviously through the miraculous power of Jesus, as the next verse declares: "So in Cana of Galilee Jesus did his first miracle. There he showed his glory, and his followers believed in him." (v. 11)

Another amazing case of matter being affected by a spirit being is found in the sizzling story of Shadrach, Meshach, and Abednego. These three men (whose original Hebrew names are Hananiah, Mishael, and Azariah) were friends of Daniel and lived among their fellow Jews during the Babylonian captivity under the authority of King Nebuchadnezzar.

There came a time when the heathen king created a giant golden statue some ninety feet high, and ordered everyone to bow down and worship the image whenever certain music was played:

> Then the man who made announcements for the king said in a loud voice, "People, nations, and those of every language, this is what you are commanded

to do: When you hear the sound of the horns, flutes, lyres, zithers, harps, pipes, and all the other musical instruments, you must bow down and worship the gold statue that King Nebuchadnezzar has set up. Anyone who doesn't bow down and worship will immediately be thrown into a blazing furnace." (Daniel 3:4-6 NCV)

How special! If people didn't wish to worship a pagan statue of gold, they'd be tossed alive into a scorching furnace. As it turns out, backstabbing Babylonian tattletales ratted out the Hebrew trio, who were not interested in worshipping the golden statue, but only the true God instead. The stool pigeons said: "O king, there are some men of Judah whom you made officers in the area of Babylon that did not pay attention to your order. Their names are Shadrach, Meshach, and Abednego. They do not serve your gods and do not worship the gold statue you have set up." (v. 12)

The king, being full of his own ego, was less than pleased when he learned of this, so he had the three men brought before him and offered them a chance to save themselves: "If you bow down and worship the statue I made, that will be good. But if you do not worship it, you will immediately be thrown into the blazing furnace. What god will be able to save you from my power then?" (v. 15)

I suspect if this were happening today, most people would simply go along with the order and bow down to the statue out of fear for their lives. But Shadrach, Meshach, and Abednego were not about to betray their faith in the Creator God, and, knowing full well that their lives were on the line, they issued one of the strongest, most inspiring statements in all of Scripture:

"Nebuchadnezzar, we do not need to defend ourselves to you. If you throw us into the blazing furnace, the God we serve is able to save us from the furnace. He will save us from your power, O king. But even if God does not save us, we want you, O king, to know this: We will not serve your gods or worship the gold statue you have set up." (vv. 16-18)

The Bible account gets very descriptive about what happened after the men told the king to, in effect, go fly a kite.

Then Nebuchadnezzar was furious with Shadrach, Meshach, and Abednego, and he changed his mind. He ordered the furnace to be heated seven times hotter than usual. Then he commanded some of the strongest soldiers in his army to tie up Shadrach, Meshach, and Abednego and throw them into the blazing furnace.

So Shadrach, Meshach, and Abednego were tied up and thrown into the blazing furnace while still wearing their robes, trousers, turbans, and other clothes. The king's command was very strict, and the furnace was made so hot that the flames killed the strong soldiers who threw Shadrach, Meshach, and Abednego into the furnace. Firmly tied, Shadrach, Meshach, and Abednego fell into the blazing furnace. (vv. 19-23)

This narrative almost sounds like a modern-day, graphic novel or big-budget movie. Three men were being tied up and tossed into a blazing furnace that was so hot, some of the soldiers escorting them were killed by the flames. But here's where the story becomes intensely intriguing. Once Shadrach, Meshach, and Abednego are tossed into the raging fire, something happens which even today is simply not explainable according to our known physical laws.

The king apparently was able to monitor the interior of this furnace, and he looked inside, expecting to see the three men screaming in agony and burning up. But instead of witnessing a human barbecue, he got an incredible shock.

> Then King Nebuchadnezzar was so surprised that he jumped to his feet. He asked the men who advised him, "Didn't we tie up only three men and throw them into the fire?" They answered, "Yes, O king." The king said, "Look! I see four men walking around in the fire. They are not tied up, and they are not burned. The fourth man looks like a son of the gods." (vv. 24-25)

Though three men had been tossed into the incinerator, they evidently found company. There was a fourth being in the form of a man walking around with the trio. This fourth being, who apparently untied the men, was said to look like a son of the gods. The King James Version says "the form of the fourth is like the Son of God."

The furnace story concludes as follows:

> Then Nebuchadnezzar went to the opening of the blazing furnace and shouted, "Shadrach, Meshach, and Abednego, come out! Servants of the Most High God, come here!" So Shadrach, Meshach, and Abednego came out of the fire. When they came out, the governors, assistant governors, captains of the soldiers, and royal advisers crowded around them and saw that the fire had not harmed their bodies. Their hair was not burned, their robes were not burned, and they didn't even smell like smoke! (vv. 26-27)

Well, now. I think it's safe to say that this event is among the most interesting miracles in the Bible. It starts with the debut in the fire of what was obviously a spirit being appearing as a man. At the very least, it was an angel, and at the most, it was Jesus Himself in another pre-birth manifestation. Remember, the King James translation says the fourth person in the blaze "is like the Son of God." So the possibility certainly exists that this was really Jesus.

What's especially fascinating is the complete control this spirit being (whether it's Jesus or an angel) had over the entire physical theater of activity. In the domain of that furnace, the spirit actually made it seem as if the fire were completely nonexistent, though everyone else continued to watch it rage.

We're told that all four men were just strolling around unfettered by their bonds while the blaze continued to burn, yet the fire did not harm them in any fashion. Their skin was not scorched. Their hair was not singed. Their clothing did not ignite. And perhaps even most stunning, they didn't even smell like smoke. Did the spirit being change the molecular structure of the fire or perhaps even the men? Or did the spirit create some sort of spirit-based shield that protected the men from anything taking place in the physical realm? The Bible never provides an answer. I've included this story here to demonstrate the astounding abilities available to those who are born of the spirit. They can actually alter the contents of what exists in the dimension where flesh dwells. (For what it's worth, notice that the fourth person in the fire never exited along with Shadrach, Meshach, and Abednego. He just apparently returned to the invisible realm of heaven.)

The point I'm stressing is that all these supernatural works—these miraculous abilities found so often in both the Old and New Testaments—are present in Scripture because God is preparing your mind for what's to come in your future. These seemingly mind-warping events that really impress us as humans now will actually become typical abilities once people have been quickened into their spirit bodies, because this is how spirit beings inherently operate. They can do what seems really impressive to our human eyes, but only because we are still physical, mortal beings with only a fraction of the knowledge and abilities we're meant to inherit.

Here's an analogy a friend once told me that may help you understand miraculous power. Let's say there's a mouse walking along the top rim of a bucket that's about half filled with water. The mouse loses its balance and plops down into the water. The rodent is able to swim around for a while, but is unable to climb out of the bucket because the sides are too slippery. Then, as the mouse runs out of energy, it begins to give up the effort and goes under. Then, all of a sudden, seemingly out of nowhere, a giant hand reaches into the bucket and plucks the mouse out by its tail and sets it down on solid ground, saving its life.

Now, in the mind of that mouse, an extraordinary miracle that it can't comprehend has just taken place. All it knows is that one moment it was drowning, and the next moment, something from somewhere rescued it from certain death and gave it another chance at living another day. But to you and me, there's nothing really miraculous about this at all. A human being simply saw the mouse struggling in the water and snatched it out. It's all in the perfectly normal course of what a person might do. There's no special ability or power involved. But by the mouse which just can't understand that, it's perceived to be a miracle.

The situation is similar with us. Right now in our human, physical, flesh-and-blood bodies, we're akin to the mouse. We don't understand precisely how events take place in that world above us and all around us—the unseen spirit dimension. We're amazed when we read about astonishing events in the Bible and think to ourselves, "Wow, what a tremendous miracle!" But to the God family and angels, this is how they operate on a daily basis. They have powers and abilities that seem mind-bending to us, but it's normal for them because, again, they are spirit beings and are not limited by the physical rules that govern our physical existence.

Yet Jesus did make a wonderful promise concerning our ability to perform great works. He said his followers would do even greater things than He performed:

> "I tell you the truth, whoever believes in me will do the same things that I do. Those who believe will do even greater things than these, because I am going to the Father." (John 14:12 NCV)

Because Jesus was resurrected and quickened by His Father to return to the spirit world, He is now opening up that world to us, one where we'll be performing even greater feats than He accomplished during His earthly ministry. It's a concept that, like God, is hard for our finite minds to grasp. You have to ask yourself, "Just how great can our works be?"

There may be no solid answer to that, because works can keep getting better and better with no definite end. But that's exactly the way things are in the spirit world. It's a dimension that's unlimited, with never-ending potential. And the Bible is clear that we in our flesh-and-blood bodies can never be part of the kingdom of God, a family of spirit beings that rule the entire seen and unseen universe. We are meant to leave these weak, mortal, corruptible, physical bodies and be quickened in an instant to become powerful, shining, immortal, incorruptible spirit beings—the glorious, divine children of God.

Chapter 3

The Kingdom of God

Now that you have a solid understanding of what we're intended to become in the future, there are important questions regarding what we're meant to be doing and where we'll be doing it. Unfortunately, even many Christians still don't understand the answers to these questions, even though they're discussed many times in Scripture. The answers have huge implications for the meaning of your life right now before the return of Jesus.

If you ask a typical believer on the street what they'll be doing for all eternity, there's a very good chance you'll hear an answer along the lines of, "I'll be spending it with Jesus, just looking at Him as I float on a cloud and play a harp. Hallelujah!"

I've asked this question of others, and a Christian woman in her twenties once told me, "I'll be looking at Jesus' face forever." I asked her again to be a little more specific about her activities year after year, decade after decade, century after century, throughout all eternity. The only answer she could come up with was, "Just looking at Jesus' face."

Don't laugh. That's actually a very common belief among people who call themselves believers, because they simply haven't grasped yet how incredible their destiny is, and how they'll be spending their time. Yes, believers will definitely get to see Jesus' face, but so many are under the mistaken impression they'll suddenly float up to their new personal address on a specific cloud and dwell forever there, strumming away on a harp or some other musical instrument, all the while praising God. Others may imagine that they'll spend their immortality in the sky, enjoying the very same activities they enjoyed during their physical lifetimes, whether it's nonstop fishing, golfing, skiing, painting, singing, shopping, lounging, snoozing, or whatever it is that floated their boat.

Please don't get me wrong. All those things sound kinda nice, but imagine doing the same thing over and over, day after day, year after year, millennia after millennia. You'd probably get a bit bored, to say the least. There are two problems with that scenario: 1) It's simply not biblical, and 2) it provides really little, if any, meaning to our challenge-filled lives here. Human beings were not designed in the image and likeness of God and put here in our temporary physical bodies to resist and overcome evil for a given number of years merely to win an atmospheric apartment on a cloud with a picturesque view of Jesus' face and an eternal round of sky golf, absent the greens fees. Sorry to burst your bubble if you happened to think that was really God's grand plan.

The Creator who made you did so with a specific purpose in mind. You've already seen that the God family is having real children, many children who will be transformed at the return of Jesus from their physical, flesh-and-blood bodies into their new divine bodies composed of spirit. These new members of the God family actually have important things to do in the kingdom of God, culminating in a paradise beyond compare.

So let's open our eyes to the inhabitants of the kingdom of God, where we're going to be, what we'll be doing, and what our surroundings will look like—subjects many lifelong Christians are confused or unclear about.

As we've seen, Jesus is returning to Earth, and that's when He'll raise His true followers from the grave, and also change any believer who happens to still be alive at the time into their new, super-deluxe, spirit bodies. It goes against the popular belief of believers existing eternally in heaven from the moment of death, but it's the truth according to Scripture. I know that many people are under the impression they instantly float up to some sort of celestial paradise of heaven, but that's simply nowhere to be found in the Good Book. What is to be found often, though, is that heaven—that is to say, the dwelling place of God—is coming here to this place we already call home, Planet Earth. There is going to be "heaven on Earth," so in that sense, people will be "in heaven" after they're raised at Jesus' return because they'll be dwelling in the same place as God's own home.

Yes, folks, the leadership of the God family is going to have a big change of venue and will relocate the headquarters of the universe out of the unseen dimension into the very visible, tangible place that we've all been dwelling in since we were born.

Initially, it'll be Jesus coming back in His long-anticipated Second Coming, setting up residence in Jerusalem, as is predicted in numerous verses:

> This is what the LORD says: "I will return to Zion and dwell in Jerusalem. Then Jerusalem will be called the Faithful City, and the mountain of the LORD Almighty will be called the Holy Mountain." (Zechariah 8:3 NIV)

"Shout and be glad, Jerusalem. I am coming, and I will live among you," says the Lord. "At that time people from many nations will join with the Lord and will become my people. Then I will live among you, and you will know that the Lord All-Powerful has sent me to you. The Lord will take Judah as his own part of the holy land, and Jerusalem will be his chosen city again. (Zechariah 2:10-12 NCV)

Moreover I will make a covenant of peace with them; it shall be an everlasting covenant with them: and I will place them, and multiply them, and will set my sanctuary in the midst of them for evermore. My tabernacle also shall be with them: yea, I will be their God, and they shall be my people. And the heathen shall know that I the LORD do sanctify Israel, when my sanctuary shall be in the midst of them for evermore. (Ezekiel 37:26-28 KJV)

It's abundantly clear that Jesus will actually make His home here on Earth, living among human beings who still need to learn God's way of life. Ezekiel indicated that even heathens (non-Christian people) will finally realize that Jesus is in charge when they see Him dwelling right in their very midst.

Moments after Jesus quickens His believers during His descent to Earth, His feet will actually land in a specific location. No, He's not going to Disney World. And, no, it's not Las Vegas or Niagara Falls either.

The Bible pinpoints the location of the ultimate touchdown as just outside Jerusalem on a hill called the Mount of Olives:

Then the Lord will go to war against those nations; he will fight as in a day of battle. On that day he will stand on the Mount of Olives, east of

> Jerusalem. The Mount of Olives will split in two,
> forming a deep valley that runs east and west. Half
> the mountain will move toward the north, and half
> will move toward the south. You will run through
> this mountain valley to the other side . . . Then the
> Lord my God will come and all the holy ones with
> him. (Zechariah 14:3-5 NCV)

The return of the King will literally be an earth-shaking experience, as a massive earthquake will split the mount, creating a large valley in the middle of it. And this is not only where Jesus will land, but also all the "holy ones," the freshly quickened believers who, as we've read in Matthew 24 and 1 Thessalonians 4, were collected by the angels in the air to meet Jesus as He is coming down to the landing place.

Incidentally, in case you never noticed this before, the spot at which Jesus returns at the Mount of Olives is the exact same place He was last seen on Earth before He ascended to heaven. That's correct. As everyone was watching Jesus float up into the sky before He vanished out of their sight, two angels dressed in white suddenly appeared to forecast His future return:

> They said, "Men of Galilee, why are you standing
> here looking into the sky? Jesus, whom you saw
> taken up from you into heaven, will come back
> in the same way you saw him go." Then they went
> back to Jerusalem from the Mount of Olives. (This
> mountain is about half a mile from Jerusalem.)
> (Acts 1:11-12 NCV)

It's uncanny how precise the Bible is, with interconnected information from books that were written centuries apart. Long before Jesus was ever born on this Earth, Zechariah of the Old Testament predicted His Second Coming would take place at the Mount of Olives, and that turned out to be the last place He stood during His First Coming (as a physical, fleshy human being) with angels announcing He'd come back to that very same location.

The notion that the kingdom of God will be present on Earth is based on more than just a single verse or two. There are many. Here's a sampling, with emphasis added so you can really see where the action of the future is going to be for God, as well as the faithful followers who will have been made immortal:

> Blessed are the meek, For they shall INHERIT THE EARTH. (Matthew 5:5 NKJV)

> Thy KINGDOM COME, Thy will be done IN EARTH, as it is in heaven. (Matthew 6:10 KJV)

> You made them to be a KINGDOM of priests for our God, and they will rule ON THE EARTH." (Revelation 5:10 NCV)

> For evildoers shall be cut off: but those that wait upon the LORD, they shall INHERIT THE EARTH. ... But the meek shall INHERIT THE EARTH; and shall delight themselves in the abundance of peace. (Psalm 37:9-11 KJV)

> For those blessed by Him shall INHERIT THE EARTH, but those cursed by Him shall be cut off. (Psalm 37:22 NKJV)

> Now it shall come to pass in the latter days That the mountain of the LORD's HOUSE Shall be established on the top of the mountains, And shall be exalted above the hills; And ALL NATIONS shall flow to it. Many people shall come and say, "Come, and let us go up to the mountain of the LORD, To the house of the God of Jacob; He will teach us His ways, And we shall walk in His paths." For out of

ZION shall go forth the law, And the word of the LORD from JERUSALEM. (Isaiah 2:2-3 NKJV)

And the LORD will be king over ALL THE EARTH. On that day there will be one LORD—his name alone will be worshiped. All the LAND from Geba, north of Judah, to Rimmon, south of Jerusalem, will become one vast plain. But JERUSALEM will be raised up in its original place and WILL BE INHABITED . . . And Jerusalem will be filled, safe at last, never again to be cursed and destroyed. (Zechariah 14:9-11 NLT)

And it shall come to pass that EVERYONE WHO IS LEFT OF ALL THE NATIONS which came against Jerusalem shall go up from year to year to worship the King, the LORD of hosts, and to keep the Feast of Tabernacles. And it shall be that whichever of the FAMILIES OF THE EARTH do not come up to JERUSALEM to worship the King, the LORD of hosts, on them there will be NO RAIN. (Zechariah 14:16-17 NKJV)

Again and again, the Bible says the kingdom of God is coming to Planet Earth, where there's plenty of land and people dwelling on that land.

Isaiah spoke of people making trips to Jerusalem, which he also calls Zion, the mountain of the Lord, and the house of the God of Jacob, to worship the Lord as well as keep the annual Feast of Tabernacles. This involves physical human beings who still don't know the laws of God making a pilgrimage to the city here on Earth to learn the way of proper living and to celebrate the eternal festivals of the Creator.

Zechariah predicted that the Jerusalem of the future would be "in its original place" and inhabited. He even gave a few extra details about people of all ages enjoying themselves in the streets of the city:

> This is what the LORD Almighty says: "Once again men and women of ripe old age will sit in the streets of Jerusalem, each of them with cane in hand because of their age. The city streets will be filled with boys and girls playing there." (Zechariah 8:4-5 NIV)

And the prophet noted that if the families of the Earth decide for whatever reason not to come up to worship Jesus in Jerusalem, they'd be plagued with God-ordained drought conditions wherever they lived. These are all physical events to happen in a physical place, Earth, which, ironically, will be run by spirit beings, the family of God! The scene is actually the opposite of what many people think is coming. They mistakenly expect believers to be physical beings spending eternity floating around the unseen dimension of heaven. But the truth is that we'll be spirit beings spending much, if not most, of our time dwelling in the visible, physical realm on Earth, engaging ourselves with human beings who are still dwelling here!

Paradise Found

I wrote earlier of the big change that believers can expect for themselves in the future, the moment they become immortal in their spirit-composed bodies. But there's also an astounding change that will happen to the Earth itself, as well as many of the living creatures that dwell on it. It's a stupendous change for the better.

Imagine for a moment some of the most inhospitable places on this planet. Perhaps the Sahara Desert, the Australian Outback, or the Siberian tundra in Russia come to mind. Imagine being stranded there without any food or water, exposed to the extremes of the elements. It's certainly a recipe for disaster. Now imagine these harsh regions being changed into something diametrically opposed to what they are, into a state that can only be described as utopia. Think of springs of pure water gushing through the arid wastelands producing a gorgeous array of flowers and other plant life. The dead zone, so to speak, suddenly teems with life.

If you think this could never happen, think again, because God says He is going to bring about such astounding changes. If you've never read the thirty-fifth chapter of Isaiah, here it is for you now. It's only ten verses long, but this majestic section of Scripture provides much information about some of the paradise-like conditions that will envelop much, if not all, of the Earth after Jesus returns:

> The desert and dry land will become happy;
> the desert will be glad and will produce flowers.
> Like a flower, it will have many blooms.
> It will show its happiness, as if it were shouting with joy.
> It will be beautiful like the forest of Lebanon,
> as beautiful as the hill of Carmel and the Plain of Sharon.
> Everyone will see the glory of the Lord
> and the splendor of our God.
> Make the weak hands strong
> and the weak knees steady.
> Say to people who are frightened,
> "Be strong. Don't be afraid.
> Look, your God will come,
> and he will punish your enemies.
> He will make them pay for the wrongs they did,
> but he will save you."
> Then the blind people will see again,
> and the deaf will hear.
> Crippled people will jump like deer,
> and those who can't talk now will shout with joy.

> Water will flow in the desert,
> and streams will flow in the dry land.
> The burning desert will have pools of water,
> and the dry ground will have springs.
> Where wild dogs once lived,
> grass and water plants will grow.
> A road will be there;
> this highway will be called "The Road to Being Holy."
> Evil people will not be allowed to walk on that road;
> only good people will walk on it.
> No fools will go on it.
> No lions will be there,
> nor will dangerous animals be on that road.
> They will not be found there.
> That road will be for the people God saves;
> the people the Lord has freed will return there.
> They will enter Jerusalem with joy,
> and their happiness will last forever.
> Their gladness and joy will fill them completely,
> and sorrow and sadness will go far away. (Isaiah 35 NCV)

It's difficult to elaborate on such a beautiful description of future conditions, but the verses mean exactly what they say. Anyone with a disability will be miraculously healed. Blind people will see, deaf people will hear, the mute will speak, and "crippled people will run like deer."

There's no question that this refers to a time after the return of Jesus, as the account specifically states "your God will come" and that "Everyone will see the glory of the Lord and the splendor of our God." Certainly, everyone has not seen the glory and splendor of God yet. Only a select few individuals since the beginning of time, such as Ezekiel and John, have already seen Jesus in His full spirit glory, and they both encountered the sight in supernatural visions. But this chapter focuses on how Jesus will reshape much of the Earth's surface, so that dry lands and deserts will be well-watered, flourishing with an abundance of magnificent flora.

The prophet Ezekiel also predicted future conditions, as he specifically addressed the people of Israel and their land, which will resemble the garden of Eden after Jesus returns:

> This is what the Sovereign LORD says: When I cleanse you from your sins, I will repopulate your cities, and the ruins will be rebuilt. The fields that used to lie empty and desolate in plain view of everyone will again be farmed. And when I bring you back, people will say, "This former wasteland is now like the Garden of Eden! The abandoned and ruined cities now have strong walls and are filled with people!" Then the surrounding nations that survive will know that I, the LORD, have rebuilt the ruins and replanted the wasteland. For I, the LORD, have spoken, and I will do what I say.
>
> "This is what the Sovereign LORD says: I am ready to hear Israel's prayers and to increase their numbers like a flock. They will be as numerous as the sacred flocks that fill Jerusalem's streets at the time of her festivals. The ruined cities will be crowded with people once more, and everyone will know that I am the LORD." (Ezekiel 36:33-38 NLT)

Once again, this forecast has not yet been fulfilled. The land of Israel is clearly not a paradise like the garden of Eden, and everyone certainly does not know that Jesus is the Lord. The passages refer to the time ahead when He comes back.

The renewal of the planet will be an impressive renovation, perhaps the greatest of all time. Here are more of the incredible details of the future conditions you'll see for yourself eventually:

"For behold, I create new heavens and a new earth;
And the former shall not be remembered or come to mind.
But be glad and rejoice forever in what I create;
For behold, I create Jerusalem as a rejoicing,
And her people a joy.
I will rejoice in Jerusalem,
And joy in My people;
The voice of weeping shall no longer be heard in her,
Nor the voice of crying.

"No more shall an infant from there live but a few days,
Nor an old man who has not fulfilled his days;
For the child shall die one hundred years old,
But the sinner being one hundred years
old shall be accursed.
They shall build houses and inhabit them;
They shall plant vineyards and eat their fruit.
They shall not build and another inhabit;
They shall not plant and another eat;
For as the days of a tree, so shall be the days of My people,
And My elect shall long enjoy the work of their hands.
They shall not labor in vain,
Nor bring forth children for trouble;
For they shall be the descendants of the blessed
of the LORD,
And their offspring with them.

"It shall come to pass
That before they call, I will answer;
And while they are still speaking, I will hear.
The wolf and the lamb shall feed together,
The lion shall eat straw like the ox,
And dust shall be the serpent's food.
They shall not hurt nor destroy in all My holy mountain,"

Says the LORD. (Isaiah 65:17-25 NKJV)

No more weeping. No more crying. No more working without a fruitful result. Requests in prayer will be answered while being made, or perhaps even beforehand. That may sound strange to people who sometimes never get an answer to their prayers now, but the Scripture plainly states, "before they call, I will answer; And while they are still speaking, I will hear."

And then there's this curious business of the nature of animals being changed. First, animal lovers have great reason to rejoice, because for those wondering if animals will be present in the kingdom, the answer is an obvious yes, with Scripture plainly stating that fact numerous times, as we're finding out. But there's more. Verse 25 notes that "The wolf and the lamb shall feed together." Now, for the sake of people who don't know much about the animal kingdom, these two critters usually don't mix well. Wolves have a nasty reputation for stalking and mercilessly devouring sheep. So for a wolf to be peacefully eating along with young sheep means that the Creator will have actually rewired their brain functions to delete the predatory nature of the wolf and make it totally tame.

In the book of Isaiah, God said this transformation would affect other animals as well, noting:

> Then wolves will live in peace with lambs,
> and leopards will lie down to rest with goats.
> Calves, lions, and young bulls will eat together,
> and a little child will lead them.
> Cows and bears will eat together in peace.
> Their young will lie down to rest together.
> Lions will eat hay as oxen do.
> A baby will be able to play near a cobra's hole,
> and a child will be able to put his hand into the
> nest of a poisonous snake.

> They will not hurt or destroy each other
> on all my holy mountain,
> because the earth will be full of the knowledge of the Lord,
> as the sea is full of water. (Isaiah 11:6-9 NCV)

This is astonishing, and goes beyond just a removal of the killing nature that many creatures currently possess. We've all seen those nature shows on television, and they're usually packed with gripping scenes of lions chasing down zebras or gazelles and then sinking their teeth into them to begin feasting on flesh. Blood starts spattering and dinner is served. But we're told that these carnivores will no longer be carnivorous. They'll suddenly be herbivores, eating plants. Lions will no longer eat the flesh of other animals, but "will eat hay as oxen do."

Even the nature of poisonous snakes will be transformed. Can you imagine allowing your precious little baby today to come within a few feet of a cobra's hole? Or letting your children stick their hands inside the nest of a poisonous snake? Yikes! The suggestion is horrific, and any parent should get a case of the willies even thinking of it. But the words on the pages of the Bible indicate that kids and vipers will apparently be best buds in the paradise conditions of the future, and children will be seen leading lions and other creatures in playtime fun!

It's even possible that the topography of the Earth will be changed, with mountain ranges as we know them seriously shaken and flattened out, creating a lot more living space and arable land for growing. We see verses that indicate:

> The mountains shake in front of him, and the
> hills melt. The earth trembles when he comes . . .
> (Nahum 1:5 NCV)

> . . . every mountain and island was moved out of its
> place. (Revelation 6:14 NKJV)

> Every valley should be raised up, and every mountain and hill should be made flat. The rough ground should be made level, and the rugged ground should be made smooth. (Isaiah 40:4 NCV)

> Then there were flashes of lightning, noises, thunder, and a big earthquake—the worst earthquake that has ever happened since people have been on earth. (Revelation 16:18 NCV)

The Bible means what it says, so we can expect serious movement of the very foundations on which we stand, and people will see giant hills appear to melt as if they had been ice cubes left outside on a warm day.

What else will change? How about the fact that there won't be any more wars or even a need for the military? I hope this doesn't disappoint those in the Armed Forces, for whom I have great respect, but everyone should be thrilled that people will no longer even be training for battle.

> The LORD will settle international disputes. All the nations will beat their swords into plowshares and their spears into pruning hooks. All wars will stop, and military training will come to an end. (Isaiah 2:4 NLT)

> Now it shall come to pass in the latter days That the mountain of the LORD's house Shall be established on the top of the mountains, And shall be exalted above the hills; And peoples shall flow to it. Many nations shall come and say, "Come, and let us go up to the mountain of the LORD, To the house of the God of Jacob; He will teach us His ways, And we shall walk in His paths." For out of Zion the law shall go forth, And the word of the LORD

from Jerusalem. He shall judge between many peoples, And rebuke strong nations afar off; They shall beat their swords into plowshares, And their spears into pruning hooks; Nation shall not lift up sword against nation, Neither shall they learn war anymore. But everyone shall sit under his vine and under his fig tree, And no one shall make them afraid; For the mouth of the LORD of hosts has spoken. (Micah 4:1-4 NKJV)

Yes, ladies and gents, world peace will finally be breaking out across the planet. It's been a dream of many diplomats and beauty-pageant contestants for countless years, and it'll finally be achieved, though not by any action of mankind. It will take the divine presence of the Creator Himself to instruct people on the ways of peace, even to the point of "rebuking them" if they continue to be belligerent. Missiles and tanks will become things of the past, as people will actually reforge the metal used in all kinds of weaponry and reuse them for farming equipment. As people travel to Jesus' dwelling place, they'll learn directly from the Prince of Peace how to establish and maintain cordial relations, so that people won't even want to go into battle. It's a far cry from a world at war with itself since the very first men and women walked the planet. People will finally be governed by the individual who created each and every one of them and wants the very best for them.

Now, even though this utopia sounds pretty darn good, and far better than the sick way the world has been run by mankind, there's still more awesomeness to come. Apparently some years after Jesus returns to Earth and sets up shop in Jerusalem, He'll eventually be joined by God the Father, who will also leave the unseen dimension of heaven and bring to Earth something known as "the New Jerusalem."

This is described near the very end of the Bible, in the second-to-last chapter of Revelation. Remember, John witnessed the future in a supernatural vision he had while living on the island of Patmos. Here's his description:

> And I saw the holy city, the new Jerusalem, coming down from God out of heaven like a beautiful bride prepared for her husband. I heard a loud shout from the throne, saying, "Look, the home of God is now among his people! He will live with them, and they will be his people. God himself will be with them. (Revelation 21:2-3 NLT)

Everyone should read those sentences again. Go ahead. Let your eyes jump back there for a few moments.

It's almost like the scene out of a science-fiction thriller, where Hollywood might depict some alien force attempting to bring its civilization from the deep recesses of outer space to our home planet, except this will be reality and with no harmful intent. It's God the Father, who looks like you and looks like me, bringing the gorgeously adorned capital city of the universe right here.

This is perhaps more significant than you might at first realize, because as mentioned previously, no human being has ever seen God the Father at any time. Not Adam, not Abraham, Isaac, or Jacob, and not Moses. Those men only saw appearances by Jesus before He was born as a human. Remember, Jesus declared that no one's ever seen God the Father:

> And the Father Himself, who sent Me, has testified of Me. You have neither heard His voice at any time, nor seen His form. (John 5:37 NKJV)

> Not that anyone has ever seen the Father; only I, who was sent from God, have seen him. (John 6:46 NLT)

And John stated:

No one has seen God at any time. (1 John 4:12 NKJV)

But here, in the final pages of the Bible, we're told that the holy city, New Jerusalem, will be brought down from heaven by God the Father, who will continue to reside in heaven even after Jesus returns to Earth, and this will be the time He'll finally join Jesus in dwelling on Earth. "Look, the home of God is now among his people! He will live with them, and they will be his people. God himself will be with them."

The New Jerusalem that God will eventually bring here will be much bigger than the city of Jerusalem today. And when I say much bigger, I mean seriously bigger, as in colossal. In fact, it's going to be of biblical proportions, literally. New Jerusalem will be a gigantic structure—possibly resembling a cube or pyramid—that stretches 1,500 miles in three dimensions. These are the specifications cited in the New Testament:

> The city was built in a square, and its length was equal to its width. The angel measured the city with the rod. The city was 1,500 miles long, 1,500 miles wide, and 1,500 miles high. (Revelation 21:16 NCV)

The King James translation of this verse says the dimensions are 12,000 furlongs in each direction. A furlong is a distance used almost exclusively these days in horse racing. One furlong is 220 yards, and there are eight furlongs in a mile. So when 12,000 furlongs are divided by eight, the result is 1,500 miles.

To put the size of this city in perspective, look at a map of the United States, and focus on the East Coast. From Maine to Florida, there are roughly 1,500 miles. So, imagine this distance stretching not only from north to south, but also east to west, heading halfway across the nation. One gigantic plot that covers a total of 2.25 million square miles.

But wait. There's more. The Bible also says the city stretches upward 1,500 miles. You read that right: 1,500 miles high. That would give the city a three-dimensional volume of 3.375 billion cubic miles, if it's indeed shaped like a cube. I know. It's simply staggering.

To give you an idea of just how high 1,500 miles is, let's do a quick comparison. Most adult human beings are between four and seven feet tall. The Statue of Liberty stands 151 feet high. New York's Empire State Building tops off at 1,250 feet. A typical hot-air balloon flight is at 2,000 feet; that's not even half of a mile high.

Bald eagles fly at 10,000 feet. The peak of Mount Everest is just over 29,000 feet, which is five and a half miles up. A typical commercial jet can be found flying at about 35,000 feet, some six to seven miles in the sky.

The higher one travels in the atmosphere, the more the gasses grow thinner, until there's no more air. At an altitude of 62 miles, you're now in outer space. NASA's space shuttles have flown at 115 to 400 miles above sea level, and the International Space Station at 200 to 250 miles. Are you beginning to get the picture yet? That's still a fraction of the 1,500 miles high the Bible indicates will be the height of the New Jerusalem. Weather and photography satellites are at 300 to 600 miles up. Spy satellites are 600 to 1,200 miles high. So the top of the dwelling place of God will definitely stretch well into the realm of what we now call outer space, where satellites are currently orbiting the planet. It won't reach the moon, though, because that's situated an average of 238,855 miles away from the Earth.

Recall how Jesus had said: "In My Father's house are many mansions; if it were not so, I would have told you. I go to prepare a place for you." (John 14:2 NKJV) This holy city that will descend from heaven, and the one to which Jesus was referring, is very likely the exact house of God the Father! The Messiah called it "My Father's house." It's where the Father of us all will eventually live on Earth, with plenty of mansions inside for all His family members who will have been made immortal!

Yes, this palatial paradise gives new meaning to the term "real estate." It'll be a jaw-dropping domicile with plenty of space for potentially everyone who has ever lived since the garden of Eden. Mathematically speaking, if everyone were to be given a quarter of a cubic mile section in which to dwell, which is a pretty good hunk of space, there'd be enough room in this giant city to accommodate 216 billion people.

John's dazzling account continues:

> . . . the city was made of pure gold, as pure as glass. The foundation stones of the city walls were decorated with every kind of jewel. The first foundation was jasper, the second was sapphire, the third was chalcedony, the fourth was emerald, the fifth was onyx, the sixth was carnelian, the seventh was chrysolite, the eighth was beryl, the ninth was topaz, the tenth was chrysoprase, the eleventh was jacinth, and the twelfth was amethyst. The twelve gates were twelve pearls, each gate having been made from a single pearl. And the street of the city was made of pure gold as clear as glass. (Revelation 21:18-21 NCV)

Many people have heard the phrase "streets paved with gold" before and think this is what it's like to be in heaven right now, but Scripture is painting the picture of a gleaming superstructure to be located in the future here on Earth. Whether the composition of the streets is the precious metal we're acquainted with or something else is a matter of speculation, because John states this gold is "as clear as glass," suggesting it's transparent. In fact, other translations use that word: "the street of the city was pure gold, like transparent glass" (v. 21 NKJV), so perhaps it's just the color of gold.

Verse 22 states, "I did not see a temple in the city, because the Lord God Almighty and the Lamb are the city's temple." (NCV) This once again demonstrates that the God family talked about in the very beginning of the gospel of John was God and the Word, for both are present in this future city, and They're referred to respectively as the Lord God Almighty and the Lamb, another name for Jesus (John 1:29). They're two different persons, but both members of the divine family of God.

We're also told that the light of celestial objects such as the sun and the moon will be irrelevant in the immediate environs of this future megaplex:

> The city does not need the sun or the moon to shine on it, because the glory of God is its light, and the Lamb is the city's lamp. By its light the people of the world will walk, and the kings of the earth will bring their glory into it. The city's gates will never be shut on any day, because there is no night there. (vv. 23-25 NCV)

Now this is illumination at its best! The light will not go away at night. For many of us, it might be difficult to envision constant light because, in this life, we're so used to the cycle of days and nights. Maybe those living in the polar extremes might be more accustomed to it, because the sun does not set there during certain times of the year. But at least in the general region of this future mammoth metropolis, the brightness of God will drown out the sunlight and extinguish the darkness, making nighttime a thing of the past.

The Government

The arrival of New Jerusalem will certainly be a phenomenal event, but long before that day, Jesus will have arrived at the Mount of Olives in what we now call Jerusalem, the one you see on television news so often, to begin the administration of what the Bible terms "the kingdom of God."

I'll take a moment here to help you understand this phrase "kingdom of God," because many people, especially those in the arena of modern religions, have been very confused by it and have tried to make it something it's not.

There are some who may think that if they just believe that God exists, then they're a part of the kingdom of God. Others might believe the kingdom is some nice, warm-and-fuzzy feeling in their hearts, knowing that they belong to God. Still others may be under the impression that if they accept God into their lives, acknowledge Jesus as their Lord and Savior, and say their prayers with real feeling, that's the kingdom of God. But none of these is correct.

The Bible uses the term "kingdom of God" dozens of times because it's telling you that there is an actual kingdom, an actual government made up of and run by God and His family. Faithful believers will be made immortal and be given very important roles to help run this government right here on Earth. I can't stress this enough: When you read the Bible, read it as you'd read any other book, where the words on the pages mean exactly what they say. Using this method makes it so much easier to understand, without having to guess about what's going to happen.

The word "kingdom" basically has two major meanings, and they both apply to this subject. The first meaning has to do with a class or ranking. You're probably already quite familiar with three famous kingdoms: the animal kingdom, the plant kingdom, and the mineral kingdom. Cats and dogs are members of the animal kingdom; trees and flowers are in the plant kingdom; and diamonds and lead are part of the mineral kingdom.

Up until now, the pages of this book have made mention of two other classes that exist in the unseen dimension of heaven: specifically the angel kingdom and the God kingdom, better known as the kingdom of God. The kingdom of God can be described as the family of God, the divine members of the *Elohim*, as put in the Hebrew language, or *Theos* in Greek, and it is expanding by having many sons and daughters born into this divine class of spirit-composed beings. They're known as the children of God.

But there's another obvious meaning for kingdom, and that is a government or area of rulership. There have been many governments throughout human history that have been called kingdoms. Even today, some political states use the K-word, such as the Kingdom of Saudi Arabia, the Kingdom of Norway, and the United Kingdom, which is headquartered in London. Kingdoms are usually defined by a people in a given region governed by a ruler or rulers who maintain order by a system of laws.

The people of the United States today may be a little less familiar with a kingdom style of government, because the country was established with a system to avoid having kings rule over citizens.

As we dive back into the Bible now, we're going to see what Scripture has to say about the kingdom of God and the important role that the quickened followers of God are meant to play.

I'll start with some of the most famous prophecies that are often read at Christmas time, when people look back at the predictions of the coming birth of Jesus and His future role:

> For unto us a Child is born, Unto us a Son is given;
> And the government will be upon His shoulder.
> And His name will be called Wonderful, Counselor,
> Mighty God, Everlasting Father, Prince of Peace. Of
> the increase of His government and peace There
> will be no end . . . (Isaiah 9:6-7 NKJV)

> "But you, Bethlehem Ephrathah, Though you are
> little among the thousands of Judah, Yet out of
> you shall come forth to Me The One to be Ruler
> in Israel, Whose goings forth are from of old, From
> everlasting." (Micah 5:2 NKJV)

> And thou Bethlehem . . . out of thee shall come
> a Governor, that shall rule my people Israel.
> (Matthew 2:6 KJV)

Many people, even those who don't happen to be Christian, are very familiar with these verses because they're not only read in churches, but have been printed on countless greeting cards, turned into songs, and sometimes even found on television as Christmas approaches.

Referring to Jesus, they talk about a child being born, a son appearing in Bethlehem, who will eventually be honored with titles such as the "Mighty God" and "Prince of Peace." But what's often overlooked in these verses is the future job description of Jesus. In case your eyes glanced right over them, Jesus is called a "ruler" and "governor," and notes that "the government will be upon His shoulder" and that "of the increase of His government" there will be no end. He's going to be the head honcho of a real, ever-expanding government, ruling over a kingdom specifically known as the kingdom of God.

Here's more, as an angel is announcing to Mary the future role of her forthcoming son:

And, behold, thou shalt conceive in thy womb, and bring forth a son, and shalt call his name JESUS. He shall be great, and shall be called the Son of the Highest: and the Lord God shall give unto him the throne of his father David: And he shall reign over the house of Jacob for ever; and of his kingdom there shall be no end. (Luke 1:31-33 KJV)

I realize that during the month of December, people hear these verses and think of a little baby lying in a manger, surrounded by shepherds and wise men (even though there were no wise men at the manger. Yes, Jesus was indeed a baby for the usual amount of time that babies are babies. But many people simply don't focus on what that baby was prophesied to do in the future a future that has still not come to pass.

Not only is Jesus called "the Son of the Highest," He is going to be given a real throne here on Earth, the throne once occupied by King David in Old Testament times, and He will "reign" in this "kingdom" that will have no end—in other words, forever. All these well-known Bible verses talk about an actual government of the future, an actual ruling kingdom that is coming to Earth out of the invisible spirit dimension of heaven.

The prophet Isaiah forecast the future rule of Jesus, saying, "Yes, the Sovereign LORD is coming in power. He will rule with a powerful arm. See, he brings his reward with him as he comes." (Isaiah 40:10 NLT)

Among the psalms of the Bible, the role of Jesus as governor of the kingdom was foretold:

He will judge the world in righteousness; he will govern the peoples with justice. (Psalm 9:8 NIV)

Oh, let the nations be glad and sing for joy! For You

shall judge the people righteously, And govern the nations on earth. (Psalm 67:4 NKJV)

The arrival of this kingdom at the Second Coming was even alluded to by one of the earliest characters of the Bible, a faithful man named Enoch, who lived seven generations after Adam. Enoch made this prediction looking ahead thousands of years, and described Jesus descending toward Earth with his quickened believers.

> "Behold, the Lord cometh with ten thousands of his saints, To execute judgment upon all, and to convince all that are ungodly among them of all their ungodly deeds which they have ungodly committed, and of all their hard speeches which ungodly sinners have spoken against him." (Jude 1:14-15 KJV)

When Jesus was being grilled by Pontius Pilate shortly before His crucifixion, He was asked if He were a king, and specifically if He were king of the Jews.

> Jesus answered, "My kingdom is not of this world. If My kingdom were of this world, My servants would fight, so that I should not be delivered to the Jews; but now My kingdom is not from here."
>
> Pilate therefore said to Him, "Are You a king then?"
>
> Jesus answered, "You say rightly that I am a king. For this cause I was born, and for this cause I have come into the world, that I should bear witness to the truth. Everyone who is of the truth hears My voice." (John 18:36-37 NKJV)

So, when pressed on the matter, Jesus did acknowledge He was a king, and, in fact, it was one of the very reasons He was born into our human world, so He could resist temptation and overcome sin, being completely obedient to the laws of God and qualifying to be the future king of the kingdom of God. He never intended to lead some political overthrow of the powers in charge during His human lifetime, even though some of His own apostles may have thought that. He was not meant to boot Caesar or any other leader from power then. Jesus' kingdom was meant for a time still ahead of us, to be brought in full force during His Second Coming when He returns as a conquering monarch, battling against human armies who will actually be fighting against Him:

> "They will make war against the Lamb, but the Lamb will defeat them, because he is Lord of lords and King of kings. He will defeat them with his called, chosen, and faithful followers." (Revelation 17:14 NCV)

Even here in Revelation, we see Jesus' role as future ruler with specific titles such as King of kings and Lord of lords. So it's abundantly clear that Jesus will be the head of the government in the coming kingdom of God.

But will Jesus be ruling alone, or will He have help? After all, Scripture does call Him the King of KINGS, and Lord of LORDS. Just who exactly are those kings and lords that the Bible talks about so majestically? Could it be God's faithful angels who will be controlling the coming kingdom with Jesus? The New Testament addresses that suggestion and rejects it outright:

> God did not choose angels to be the rulers of the new world that was coming, which is what we have been talking about. (Hebrews 2:5 NCV)

Just a few lines earlier, the same book mentions the true role of angels: "All the angels are spirits who serve God and are sent to help those who will receive salvation." (Hebrews 1:14 NCV)

Yes, folks, angels are meant to serve those who will receive salvation—in other words, serving *us*, the people obedient to God who will eventually be born into God's own family for an amazing purpose. That purpose provides the answer to the question of who will be helping Jesus rule in the kingdom. It's one of the most invigorating aspects of the divine secret, finally giving so much meaning to the trials and tribulations of this life.

The kings of the future, the lords who will reign and rule under the authority of Jesus Christ, are none other than the faithful believers who have undergone the change from mortal to immortal, from flesh to spirit, from the human family to the divine family. They are the saved children of God, the quickened believers now part of God's own family. This is among the most important messages of the entire Bible, and is, ironically, one of the least known.

Now you might be thinking to yourself, "What? Was I really born to reign and rule with the Creator of the universe? There's just no bleeping way, man." I admit it can sound a bit strange at first, but the biblical answer is a resounding "Yes! You *were* born to rule!"

Just take a look at these astonishing quotes from the Bible. It makes no difference which translation you prefer. Any and all versions indicate the same thing. I'm adding emphasis to some of the words just to make sure you don't miss the point of what's coming in your very own future if you're one of God's servants.

> If we endure, We shall also REIGN with Him. (2 Timothy 2:12 NKJV)

> And he that overcometh, and keepeth my works unto the end, to him will I give POWER OVER THE NATIONS: And he shall RULE THEM with a rod of iron; as the vessels of a potter shall they be broken to shivers: even as I received of my Father. (Revelation 2:26-27 KJV)

Then I saw some THRONES AND PEOPLE SITTING ON THEM WHO HAD BEEN GIVEN THE POWER TO JUDGE. And I saw the souls of those who had been killed because they were faithful to the message of Jesus and the message from God. They had not worshiped the beast or his idol, and they had not received the mark of the beast on their foreheads or on their hands. THEY CAME BACK TO LIFE AND RULED WITH CHRIST for a thousand years. (The others that were dead did not live again until the thousand years were ended.) This is the first raising of the dead. Blessed and holy are those who share in this first raising of the dead. The second death has no power over them. They will be priests for God and for Christ and will RULE WITH HIM for a thousand years. (Revelation 20:4-6 NCV)

Thou art worthy to take the book, and to open the seals thereof: for thou wast slain, and hast redeemed us to God by thy blood out of every kindred, and tongue, and people, and nation; And hast MADE US unto our God, KINGS, and priests: and WE SHALL REIGN ON THE EARTH. (Revelation 5:9-10 KJV)

TO HIM WHO OVERCOMES I WILL GRANT TO SIT WITH ME ON MY THRONE, as I also overcame and sat down with My Father on His throne. (Revelation 3:21 NKJV)

I hope you're not about to drift off into snoozeland. This is no time for a nap because these Bible verses are nothing short of eye-popping. They're explaining to you in very clear terms your personal future if you're one who overcomes the ways of the world and truly follows the ways of the Creator.

These Bible verses say Jesus will have made us—the quickened believers who come back to life—*kings*. They say He's going to give us *power over the nations*. They say we're going to *rule* those nations with a rod of iron, which is like a "you better behave, or else you get whacked" method. They say we're going to rule with Jesus for a thousand years. They say we're going to *reign* right here on the Earth. They say we're going to sit down on the throne of the member of the God family named Jesus Christ, just as Jesus has sat down with God the Father on His throne.

And just in case you think this terminology is some book-of-Revelation-style language that's not meant to be taken literally, it's also repeated by the prophet Daniel, who was also given advance notice of what would happen with the return of Jesus:

> But the holy people who belong to the Most High God will receive the POWER TO RULE and will have the POWER TO RULE FOREVER, from now on. (Daniel 7:18 NCV, emphasis added)

> Then the holy people who belong to the Most High God will have the POWER TO RULE. They will RULE OVER ALL THE KINGDOMS under heaven with power and greatness, and THEIR POWER TO RULE WILL LAST FOREVER. People from all the other kingdoms will respect and serve them. (v. 27 NCV, emphasis added)

In fact, if you stop and think about it for a moment, the very first book of the Bible indicates that men and women were placed here to begin with so they could learn *how to rule* over everything on the planet, to properly take care of all living things.

> Then God said, "Let us make human beings in our image and likeness. And LET THEM RULE over the fish in the sea and the birds in the sky, over the tame animals, over all the earth, and over all

the small crawling animals on the earth." (Genesis
1:26 NCV, emphasis added)

Isn't it about time you read and accepted the incredible future
that is meant for you? The Bible continually talks about the
resurrected believers who belong to God being given the power
to rule—not just over animals, but over nations that still exist
here on Earth.

The Bible even names names of some of the people we'll see
in the kingdom, and sometimes mentions rulership roles. For
instance, we know that Abraham, Isaac, and Jacob and every
single prophet of God will be there, because Jesus said so: ". . .
you will see Abraham, Isaac, Jacob, and all the prophets within
the Kingdom of God . . ." (Luke 13:28 NLT)

We know that King David will be resurrected from the dead
and be given a role as a king in the kingdom, specifically over
the twelve tribes of Israel. We know this because long after David
died, God predicted his role as a ruler of the future:

> But they shall serve the LORD their God, And
> David their king, Whom I will raise up for them.
> (Jeremiah 30:9 NKJV)

> My servant David will be their king, and they will all
> have one shepherd. They will live by my rules and
> obey my laws. They will live on the land I gave to
> my servant Jacob, the land in which your ancestors
> lived. They will all live on the land forever: they,
> their children, and their grandchildren. David my
> servant will be their king forever. (Ezekiel 37:24-25
> NCV)

Just so you don't miss it, the prophecy noted that David will be
their king forever, obviously referring to the eternal kingdom of
God that's still ahead. He'll be among those resurrected to spirit

life to help in the rulership of God's future kingdom. There's no other way to construe this, especially because David was dead and buried when this was originally written.

And if by chance you're one of those people under the impression that God's laws have been done away with, the prophecy shows that's not the case at all, as God explained, "They will live by my rules and obey my laws." This notion is echoed countless times in Scripture, as Paul explained, "For not the hearers of the law are just before God, but the DOERS of the law shall be justified." (Romans 2:13 KJV, emphasis added) Jesus Himself taught that not the tiniest bit of God's law was being abolished, as He stressed, "Whoever refuses to obey any command and teaches other people not to obey that command will be the least important in the kingdom of heaven. But whoever obeys the commands and teaches other people to obey them will be great in the kingdom of heaven." (Matthew 5:19 NCV)

Other characters likely to have high positions in the kingdom are the twelve apostles of Jesus, because the New Jerusalem will have their names engraved on the city's exterior walls, and Jesus said they would all be judging from thrones:

> The walls of the city were built on twelve foundation stones, and on the stones were written the names of the twelve apostles of the Lamb. (Revelation 21:14 NCV)

> And you will sit on thrones, judging the twelve tribes of Israel. (Luke 22:30 NCV)

If you read the entire eleventh chapter of the Book of Hebrews, there's a list of what I like to call Bible All-Stars. They're people singled out for their outstanding faith during their human lifetimes. Included among these all-stars are Moses, Joseph, Noah, Enoch, Abel, Abraham, Isaac, Jacob, Sarah, David, and Samson. Scripture also mentions that when all of these Old Testament heroes and heroines died, they did *not* receive any of the fantastic promises, including eternal life. Yet they knew all the good stuff would eventually come their way:

> All these great people died in faith. They did not get the things that God promised his people, but they saw them coming far in the future and were glad. (Hebrews 11:13 NCV)

The text comes right out and plainly states that the reward was to be inherited far into the future. This, of course, underscores the fact that these champions of God will all be resurrected and receive the promise of immortal life and co-rulership with their spiritual brother Jesus at His Second Coming.

The chapter also notes that "Abraham was waiting for the city that has real foundations—the city planned and built by God" (v. 10) and that "God is not ashamed to be called their God, because he has prepared a city for them." (v. 16) The city being referred to is the New Jerusalem that is planned and built by God, and coming to Earth to be the eventual headquarters of the kingdom.

I mentioned earlier how angels are not the ones who'll be the rulers of the future. It'll be the quickened believers known as the children of God. But there's something about angels that even many longtime Christians don't realize, despite it being unmistakably declared by the apostle Paul. He said that in the coming kingdom, believers will be judging angels, and judging the citizens of the world. This is exactly how the Bible talks about your future job:

> Don't you know that someday we Christians are going to judge the world? And since you are going to judge the world, can't you decide these little things among yourselves? Don't you realize that we Christians will judge angels? (1 Corinthians 6:2-3 NLT)

These verses of Scripture are simply stunning! Many don't realize that when it comes to the classes of beings that God created, men and women were made in a division just under the angels, at least for a little while. But in the future, they'll be above the angels, because they'll be born into the God family.

> For somewhere in the Scriptures it says, "What is man that you should think of him, and the son of man that you should care for him? FOR A LITTLE WHILE you made him lower than the angels, and you crowned him with glory and honor. You gave him authority over ALL THINGS." Now when it says "all things," it means nothing is left out. But we have not yet seen all of this happen. (Hebrews 2:6-8 NLT, emphasis added)

Human beings are currently "lower than the angels," but only for a little while. That "little while" is our human lifespan, the time spent in our physical, made-out-of-flesh bodies, no matter how long we live. But this very same section of Scripture also says we're to be crowned in the future with glory, honor, and "authority over all things." And to make sure you're getting the picture of what is meant by "all things," Scripture goes on to explain that "nothing is left out." "All things" means all created things. Everything. The entire universe. We just haven't seen this change take place yet. It's all coming, though. The Bible clearly indicates that people who were once ordinary human beings, the kind who put their pants on one leg at a time, are designed ultimately to have authority and rulership over every created thing, including the citizens of the world and even over angels!

As you know, Jesus often spoke in parables when discussing the coming kingdom of God, and one of His stories provides some very vivid clues about how the government is going to be structured. Here's the analogy in its entirety before I highlight a few key points:

The crowd was listening to everything Jesus said. And because he was nearing Jerusalem, he told a story to correct the impression that the Kingdom of God would begin right away.

He said, "A nobleman was called away to a distant empire to be crowned king and then return.

Before he left, he called together ten servants and gave them ten pounds of silver to invest for him while he was gone. But his people hated him and sent a delegation after him to say they did not want him to be their king.

When he returned, the king called in the servants to whom he had given the money. He wanted to find out what they had done with the money and what their profits were. The first servant reported a tremendous gain—ten times as much as the original amount!

'Well done!' the king exclaimed. 'You are a trustworthy servant. You have been faithful with the little I entrusted to you, so you will be governor of ten cities as your reward.'"

The next servant also reported a good gain—five times the original amount.

'Well done!' the king said. 'You can be governor over five cities.'

"But the third servant brought back only the original amount of money and said, 'I hid it and kept it safe. I was afraid because you are a hard man to deal with, taking what isn't yours and harvesting crops you didn't plant.'

" 'You wicked servant!' the king roared. 'Hard, am I? If you knew so much about me and how tough I am, why didn't you deposit the money in the bank so I could at least get some interest on it?' Then turning to the others standing nearby, the king ordered, 'Take the money from this servant, and give it to the one who earned the most.'

" 'But, master,' they said, 'that servant has enough already!'

" 'Yes,' the king replied, 'but to those who use well what they are given, even more will be given. But from those who are unfaithful, even what little they have will be taken away. And now about these enemies of mine who didn't want me to be their king—bring them in and execute them right here in my presence.' " (Luke 19:11-27 NLT)

All right. The first thing worth discussing is why Jesus told this parable to begin with. Luke indicated it was to correct the false impression that the kingdom of God would begin right away. I can't stress this enough, because so many people even today believe the false notion that the kingdom is here now, or that it started when Jesus was walking the Earth. Neither of those beliefs is correct. Many people pray on a daily basis, "Thy kingdom come," but they don't realize what they're calling on God to do. They're actually requesting that God bring the kingdom to Earth, because it's not here yet. Everyone needs to face the fact that the Holy Bible says that God's kingdom is not starting right away. It's meant for a later time in the future, once Jesus returns. Remember also that Jesus Himself stated, "My kingdom is not of this world." (John 18:36 NKJV)

This parable also confirms the timetable, because the nobleman it's talking about is really referring to Jesus. He "was called away to a distant empire to be crowned king and then return." This is a direct metaphor for Jesus being quickened by His Father out of the grave, being crowned king in the unseen "empire" of heaven, and His eventual return to assume His future role as king of the kingdom on Earth.

The remainder of the story focuses on the actions of the nobleman's servants, each of whom had been given ten pounds of silver to invest. The ones who invested wisely saw the money grow, and they were ultimately rewarded by the nobleman. And what was their reward? Floating on clouds with harps? No, it was governing cities!

The servant who saw a ten-fold increase in his pile of precious metal was specifically told, "You will be governor of ten cities as your reward." And the servant who saw a five-fold increase in his silver was told that he, too, had done a fine job and that he can be "governor over five cities." The story is speaking of how governing authority will be allotted in the kingdom. Some will receive more than others, depending on what they did in this lifetime, but it all has to do with the administration of the government of God.

Jesus used this parable and a similar one involving talents in the twenty-fifth chapter of Matthew to let us know that what we do with the information and abilities God has given us will be factored into our reward, which again includes governorship, rulership, and authority over certain areas and people in the coming kingdom. The more that we do with the gifts God has given us now, the more responsibility we will apparently have in the future kingdom.

Yes, God the Father and Jesus Christ will still be the ultimate ones in charge, but we need to understand that They're granting us a certain amount of co-rulership with Them. If we would wake up to the glorious destiny thus intended for us, we'd have the answers to so many questions about why we're alive and what the real meaning of life is.

Life Does Have Meaning

From the time we're young children to the final moments of our existence, we as human beings wonder why we're all here and what it's all about. For those who think that the universe and life on Earth are just some accident resulting from the flatulence of cosmic gas, there really is no meaning. They presume we're just the product of some ancient "What the heck was that?" moment, where there's no Creator, no Designer, no God, and that everything was formulated by nothingness. How ridiculous. The Bible actually calls people who think that way fools. After all, "The fool has said in his heart, 'There is no God.'" (Psalm 14:1 NKJV)

But even for the non-fools among us who do believe in the existence of God—the God of the Bible—and proudly declare themselves to be Christians, countless millions still have little idea what life is truly all about. They live day to day under the assumption that if they acknowledge the existence of God, accept Jesus as their Lord and Savior, and then generally live a good life, they're on their way to an eternity of doing pretty much nothing but strumming a harp while living on a cloud in heaven, gazing at the face of Jesus. Oh, and of course, throw a *hallelujah* and *amen* in there for good measure.

That paradigm simply does not answer all of the "why" questions in everyone's life. Why are we all here? Why is life so challenging? What is God really doing with us anyway? Why all the trouble, hardship, persecution, famine, nakedness, and threats of death? Why can't Christians experience paradise right now?

There's a reason why we were all brought into existence, and it has nothing to do with the famous cliché, "Whoever dies with the most toys wins." It's not even about experiencing the most enjoyment possible. There's a reason why life seems hard at times. There's a reason why becoming a Christian is not like waving a magic wand and suddenly life becomes an instant utopia of ease and relaxation. To the contrary, making the conscious decision to follow the God of the Bible usually makes life much more challenging and difficult.

Knowing what one's true destiny is and what God is really doing with us is crucial to understanding the purpose and meaning behind all of this. The answer has to do with the fact that human beings are indeed meant to be transformed into the divine family of God and become the co-rulers of the future. But we need to be thoroughly prepared and made ready for that change. We actually have to have our minds and attitudes prepared as we learn to follow God's way of life instead of our own. We need our character to be properly developed and perfected to become spiritually mature, just like the character of the divine family, because we'll be spending all of eternity dwelling with Them, doing the very things They do.

Believe it or not, creation did not end in the garden of Eden. It was just beginning. God's greatest creation—His masterpiece work, as the Bible terms it—is continuing right this second, inside those people who have joined themselves to their Maker. "For we are God's masterpiece. He has created us anew in Christ Jesus, so we can do the good things he planned for us long ago." (Ephesians 2:10 NLT) We are new creations with Jesus inside us, and we're intended to do the good things planned for us way back in the ancient recesses of time, before Adam and Eve were created.

While human beings are fashioned in the same general form and shape as God, we're not born into this world with the consummate character of God already embedded in us. We're not initially made complete, but we are intended to become complete and mature. We're not formed with the automatic volition to be obedient, righteous individuals. Yet we can learn to be that way. We begin our lives with something we call human nature. The Bible terms it sinful nature, a mind of the flesh, or a carnal mind, depending on the translation. Scripture also declares that this nature is actually "hostile to God."

> Those who are dominated by the sinful nature think about sinful things, but those who are controlled by the Holy Spirit think about things that please the Spirit. If your sinful nature controls your mind, there is death. But if the Holy Spirit controls your mind, there is life and peace. For the sinful nature is always hostile to God. It never did obey God's laws, and it never will. That's why those who are still under the control of their sinful nature can never please God. (Romans 8:5-8 NLT)

This is where the rubber meets the road, folks. We simply cannot be like God and please our Creator when we're dominated and controlled by our sinful nature. Remember that sin is the breaking of God's law (1 John 3:4). The purpose of our lives in the flesh right now is to learn, with our Creator's assistance, how to battle against and overcome human nature—the carnal mind, the sinful, rebellious way that's hostile to God, and become more like God in character by not only following the instructions of God, but *desiring* them as well.

Just having a desire in one's heart to do the commandments goes a long way with our Creator, who said: "I wish their hearts would always respect me and that they would always obey my commands so that things would go well for them and their children forever!" (Deuteronomy 5:29 NCV)

One of the wisest men who ever lived, King Solomon, summed it up this way: "Fear God, and keep his commandments: for this is the whole duty of man." (Ecclesiastes 12:13 KJV)

By honoring God and keeping His commandments, we're learning the way the divine family lives. We're practicing day after day, week after week, year after year how to live like God, to get ourselves ready for never-ending years of living in the same family. This temporary, mortal, physical existence we all share is practice and preparation for the future. Consider it a "training session" for the stupendous eternity ahead.

The Bible even uses words such as "train" and "exercise," telling us to prepare ourselves for the lifestyle of God:

> . . . train yourself to be godly. "Physical training is good, but training for godliness is much better, promising benefits in this life and in the life to come." (1 Timothy 4:7-8 NLT)

> . . . exercise yourself toward godliness. For bodily exercise profits a little, but godliness is profitable for all things, having promise of the life that now is and of that which is to come. (NKJV)

All of the challenges, troubles, trials, and tribulations we experience in this life are here intentionally as a form of instruction, practice, training, and resistance to help us develop our godly character for our future roles in the eternal kingdom. Many people forget that Scripture tells us to resist everything from the devil. "Resist the devil, and he will flee from you." (James 4:7 KJV)

Just as athletes, singers, and musicians need training, practice, and rehearsal to reach their optimum performance level, so we need to practice constantly to learn how to select God's way instead of our own rebellious path. Just as a weightlifter keeps adding weight for more resistance to develop more strength, resistance in the form of suffering, hardship, and persecution actually helps us develop our character, humbling our egos and heightening the desire and know-how to do what's correct. We're simply not manufactured like assembly-line robots pre-programmed to do the right thing automatically. We need to learn how to desire and choose the right thing in spite of all the heartache, grief, and evil we experience. Scripture prominently declares:

> Today I have given you the choice between life and death, between blessings and curses. Now I call on heaven and earth to witness the choice you make. Oh, that you would choose life, so that you and your descendants might live! You can make this choice by loving the LORD your God, obeying him, and committing yourself firmly to him. This is the key to your life. (Deuteronomy 30:19-20 NLT)

We're told the key to life is loving and obeying God, making that firm commitment. Our Creator is begging us to choose life after becoming aware of both pathways, the ways that lead to eternal life and eternal death. We're meant to learn how to resist the evil and opt for the good. In a very strong sense, we're in school at the present time. We're being thoroughly taught and prepared, learning how to live like God because we're intended to join that divine, spirit-composed family as the children of God.

As an analogy, when we attend elementary school, high school, or college, not only do we receive instruction, but we're allowed to make mistakes so we can learn from those errors and get the answers correct in the future. On the path toward higher education and eventual graduation, we're continually tested in class with more challenging and difficult problems to make sure we're growing intellectually.

In parallel manner with our present lives, God provides us instruction and allows us to make mistakes so we can learn from them, abandoning our harmful behavior and moving toward the godly way of life. The challenges and problems we face often get tougher as we progress, because God, who is sometimes described as a potter (Jeremiah 18:6, Romans 9:21), is testing, molding, shaping, and improving us like clay, helping us grow in character as we walk along the path toward our graduation into glory, our future role as immortal rulers in the government of God.

Now consider this for a moment. If your current life were totally fantastic, with smooth sailing for you every single day without a challenge of any kind or care in the world, do you think your mind and desires would just naturally gravitate toward obeying God in every way possible? Do you think you'd learn how to be an overcomer of anything? If you think the answer is yes, you're fooling yourself. The truth is, your mind would gravitate away from God and you probably wouldn't even be aware of it. You'd be filled with endless distractions. The sinful nature that's within every single one of us is like a space-age tractor beam or gravitational force that's actually pulling us away from becoming godly. It keeps our minds occupied with anything and everything except obedience to our Creator because it's hostile to God. But while the Bible says that our sinful nature urges us to act a certain evil way, there's hope for all of us because Scripture also promises we can resist and overcome it with the help of God's own Spirit.

During one of Jesus' earliest recorded appearances, He personally talked with Adam and Eve's son, Cain, telling him he could win his personal battle with disobedience. He encouraged Cain to subdue and master the sinful nature:

> The Lord asked Cain, "Why are you angry? Why do you look so unhappy? If you do things well, I will accept you, but if you do not do them well, sin is ready to attack you. Sin wants you, but you must rule over it." (Genesis 4:6-7 NCV)

Paul elaborated on this theme in the New Testament:

> So, dear brothers and sisters, you have no obligation whatsoever to do what your sinful nature urges you to do. For if you keep on following it, you will perish. But if through the power of the Holy Spirit you turn from it and its evil deeds, you will live. For all who are led by the Spirit of God are children of

God. So you should not be like cowering, fearful slaves. You should behave instead like God's very own children, adopted into his family—calling him "Father, dear Father." For his Holy Spirit speaks to us deep in our hearts and tells us that we are God's children. And since we are his children, we will share his treasures—for everything God gives to his Son, Christ, is ours, too. But if we are to share his glory, we must also share his suffering. Yet what we suffer now is nothing compared to the glory he will give us later. (Romans 8:12-18 NLT)

Here Paul clearly said we don't have to do what our sinful nature is urging us to do. We're not being forced. We can resist evil with the help of the very power of God—the Holy Spirit—and that's the path that leads to immortality and receiving everything the Father has given to Jesus. It's a perfection process that takes effort and time, sometimes an entire lifetime of practice and preparation, but something Scripture constantly instructs us to pursue: "Therefore, since we have these promises, dear friends, let us purify ourselves from everything that contaminates body and spirit, PERFECTING HOLINESS out of reverence for God." (2 Corinthians 7:1 NIV, emphasis added) Truly, practice makes for perfection.

Paul also touched on the reason there is suffering in our lives. He explained that, in order to share the glory that Christ has, we're meant to experience what our Creator Jesus experienced, and—like it or not—that includes suffering and persecution. That theme was repeated in the book of Acts, where Paul and Barnabas both stated, "We must suffer many things to enter God's kingdom." (Acts 14:22 NCV)

Becoming a literal child of God is not a carefree, easy process for us. Even though we are saved by grace as a free gift from

God (Ephesians 2:8), Jesus also said that when He returns, He "will reward each person according to what they have done." (Matthew 16:27 NIV) And part of what needs to be done in life is learning to overcome pain and adversity and still remain faithful, obedient servants to God. It is beneficial exercise for our character development, to refine us and help in the perfection process so we become more like the Creator who fashioned us in the first place. It surprises many people that Jesus Himself had to go through this suffering-to-be-perfected process for both His own benefit and for ours in the long run:

> He learned obedience by the things which He suffered. And having been perfected, He became the author of eternal salvation to all who obey Him ... (Hebrews 5:8-9 NKJV)

Yes, as stunning as it may seem, Jesus Christ was perfected by having to endure suffering, thus learning obedience. Scripture says God the Father "made the One who leads people to salvation perfect through suffering." (Hebrews 2:10 NCV)

I just can't stress this enough: The Savior of mankind was Himself perfected through suffering! So how much more do we, as sinful human beings, need to experience it? According to Peter, believers should even *expect* to suffer in life, because it can act as an attitude-improver, waking us up to the need for obedience to God's laws, instead of pursuing whatever our covetous hearts desire:

> So then, since Christ suffered physical pain, you must arm yourselves with the same attitude he had, and be ready to suffer, too. For if you have suffered physically for Christ, you have finished with sin. You won't spend the rest of your lives chasing your own desires, but you will be anxious to do the will of God. (1 Peter 4:1-2 NLT)

Suffering is an attention-getter that quickly humbles us, and Peter was explaining that once believers have suffered, they would finally stop running after their own desires, and instead follow God completely. And as strange as it may sound, Jesus' own brother James said Christians should not feel dejected when they suffer troubles in life, but *thrilled*:

> Dear brothers and sisters, when troubles come your way, consider it an opportunity for great joy. For you know that when your faith is tested, your endurance has a chance to grow. So let it grow, for when your endurance is fully developed, you will be perfect and complete, needing nothing. (James 1:2-4 NLT)

It's quite clear that God wants to thoroughly test us to shape and perfect us as complete individuals. The Master Potter is not just playing around with clay for fun. He has a stellar, finished product in mind. He wants us truly behaving in the way the God family behaves. A prime example of a divine test can be found in the four decades that God had His own people, Israel, spend in the wilderness before guiding them into the Promised Land. He, of course, could have brought the people to their destination much sooner than forty years, but Scripture tells us outright the entire venture was one giant test:

> Remember how the Lord your God has led you in the desert for these forty years, taking away your pride and testing you, because he wanted to know what was in your heart. He wanted to know if you would obey his commands. (Deuteronomy 8:2 NCV)

The same holds true today. The test for all of us continues. God still wants to know what's really in our heart, and whether you and I will obey His eternal laws, the instructions for living spelled out in the Bible. They outline the only way of life for those in the divine family. Because we're meant to be dwelling forever in that same family, God wants to make sure we're living the proper way, and that we *desire* to live in that fashion. This is why the Bible is filled with instructions and commands for us on how to live. They're not included to put a damper on all the so-called "fun" people think they can have by disobeying them. They're designed for our benefit, not only in this temporary physical lifetime, but in the everlasting, spirit-composed kingdom of God in the future. God is so serious about our obedience, Scripture calls us LIARS if we claim to know God but don't follow the divine commands:

> We can be sure that we know God if we obey his commands. Anyone who says, "I know God," but does not obey God's commands is a liar, and the truth is not in that person. But if someone obeys God's teaching, then in that person God's love has truly reached its goal. This is how we can be sure we are living in God: Whoever says that he lives in God must live as Jesus lived. (1 John 2:3-6 NCV)

Unfortunately, many people are under the mistaken impression that if they simply proclaim that Jesus is their Savior, then they instantly lock themselves in for eternal salvation and are granted an entry ticket to the kingdom of God. But Jesus made it clear that's not the case at all:

> "Not everyone who calls out to me, 'Lord! Lord!' will enter the Kingdom of Heaven. Only those who actually do the will of my Father in heaven will enter. On judgment day many will say to me, 'Lord! Lord! We prophesied in your name and cast out demons in your name and performed many miracles in your name.' But I will reply, 'I never knew you.

> Get away from me, you who break God's laws.' "
> (Matthew 7:21-23 NLT)

Yes, you're reading that correctly. There are *many* believers in Christ who will claim they prophesied in the name of Jesus and were able to cast out demons and perform many miracles, and yet the Creator of the universe will tell them to go away, that He never knew them. Remember that Jesus taught, "If you love Me, keep My commandments." (John 14:15 NKJV) Apparently, there is something far more important in the salvation process than just acknowledging or even publicly declaring faith in Jesus. It is actually **doing His will, following His instructions, and not breaking the eternal laws of God!** James reminded everyone: "You say you have faith, for you believe that there is one God. Good for you! **Even the demons believe this, and they tremble in terror.**" (James 2:19 NLT, emphasis added) Accepting God into our lives is not the end of the process. It's merely the beginning. To receive the magnificent, priceless gift of admission into the divine family, we need to be thoroughly prepared and to be made complete. God the Father and Jesus aren't just *having* children, they're *raising* them as well!

Now let's go back briefly to the issue of having to suffer trials and tribulations. Jesus warned the members of His church in Smyrna that they would suffer and possibly even be killed, but at the same time told them not to fear such a result: "Do not be afraid of what you are about to suffer. I tell you, the devil will put some of you in prison to test you, and you will suffer for ten days. But be faithful, even if you have to die, and I will give you the crown of life." (Revelation 2:10 NCV)

Jesus endured and overcame all the suffering presented to Him, even to the point of an excruciating death, and thus qualified for His role as King of kings. We, too, are those kings, the actual children of God, sharing Christ's own glory. Having said that, the problems we face in our lives today—even if they concern our own death—will seem like nothing compared to the awesomeness coming our way as the literal brothers and sisters of the universe's Creator. As Paul said:

> For our present troubles are small and won't last very long. Yet they produce for us a glory that vastly outweighs them and will last forever! So we don't look at the troubles we can see now; rather, we fix our gaze on things that cannot be seen. For the things we see now will soon be gone, but the things we cannot see will last forever. (2 Corinthians 4:17-18 NLT)

Yes, it's a mind-blowing purpose, but God is a mind-blowing, limitless God. And the divine family is urging us to get our act together so we can be properly prepared for thinking, living, and acting in the glory-filled kingdom to come. If we can successfully do that, we can teach others how to do the same.

That's correct. It ain't just about us. It's about other people and their benefit. We need to learn in this life how to overcome the harmful ways of living so we can properly instruct others on how to do the same when we help govern and judge the nations in the coming kingdom of God. It's perhaps more about the future than it is about the present. This temporary, mortal, physical life is just a training session for the marvelous, everlasting kingdom ahead!

You're probably already aware that a common theme throughout the Bible is that our way of life is intended to focus on the well-being of other people. The famous ancient question was asked by Adam's son, Cain: "Am I my brother's keeper?" (Genesis 4:9 NKJV) The answer was not given immediately, but in a way, the entire rest of the Bible provides a resounding *yes* to that question.

In both the Old and New Testaments, Jesus told us to "love your neighbor as yourself." (Leviticus 19:18, Matthew 22:39 NKJV) He also said, "Do to others what you would want them to do to you." (Luke 6:31 NCV) The apostle John put it this way: "This is the message you heard from the beginning: We should love one another." (1 John 3:11 NIV)

Additionally, Jesus instructed us to care not only for people we tend to like, but also those we tend not to like, specifically our enemies:

> But love your enemies, do good to them, and lend to them without hoping to get anything back. Then you will have a great reward, and you will be children of the Most High God, because he is kind even to people who are ungrateful and full of sin. (Luke 6:35 NCV)

> "You have heard that it was said, 'Love your neighbor and hate your enemy.' But I tell you, love your enemies and pray for those who persecute you, that you may be children of your Father in heaven. He causes his sun to rise on the evil and the good, and sends rain on the righteous and the unrighteous. If you love those who love you, what reward will you get? Are not even the tax collectors doing that? And if you greet only your own people, what are you doing more than others? Do not even pagans do that? Be perfect, therefore, as your heavenly Father is perfect. (Matthew 5:43-48 NIV)

Once again, Jesus Himself instructed us to be perfect, and part of that perfection and completeness includes loving all others, including our enemies. It's an attitude we don't have naturally instilled in us. The command has perplexed many over the centuries. Some have undoubtedly thought, and perhaps still think, that we should actually hate and get rid of our enemies. But part of our growth process is to become more like God in righteous character, caring for people who don't care for us.

It's a portion of the wondrous plan for the future, because the God family loves and cares even for those who don't love Them, sending blessings to even disobedient people. It's a prominent indicator of one of the most enthralling and mysterious aspects of the divine secret I have not mentioned to this point: a likely future chance for even non-believers to repent and join God's family as well.

Good News!
There's Hope for Others

Yes, as incredible as it may seem, God the Father and Jesus Christ are not bent on destroying countless millions and even billions of people They created in Their own image who have never really understood the truth or simply never even heard it depending on the country or the period in which they lived They're not looking to torture or permanently snuff out the lives of countless little children in faraway, pagan-dominated lands who never heard the name of Jesus and instead worshipped nonexistent gods because their parents were misinformed. God actually wants to save them and will likely give them the opportunity, but in a time frame determined by the Father and Jesus.

I don't wish at all to imply that God is unwilling to destroy people. He most certainly is. Jesus Himself said twice that "unless you repent you will all likewise perish." (Luke 13:3,5 NKJV) Repentance, which is turning away from disobedience to follow the ways of God, is the key to not perishing. And perishing means exactly what you think it means. Nonexistence. Everlasting destruction. Total death.

Jesus wasn't referring to the initial death everyone typically faces, because even the most faithful heroes of the Bible all died. He was referring to perishing forever, the second death, the eternal death from which there is no more resurrection. The Bible, in explicit terms, does talk about a *second* death in a lake of fire that's set to completely consume those who refuse to repent.

> But the cowardly, the unbelieving, the vile, the murderers, the sexually immoral, those who practice magic arts, the idolaters and all liars— their place will be in the fiery lake of burning sulfur. This is the second death." (Revelation 21:8 NIV)

> And anyone whose name was not found written in the book of life was thrown into the lake of fire. (Revelation 20:15 NCV)

> For, behold, the day cometh, that shall burn as an oven; and all the proud, yea, and all that do wickedly, shall be stubble: and the day that cometh shall burn them up, saith the LORD of hosts, that it shall leave them neither root nor branch. . . . And ye shall tread down the wicked; for they shall be ashes under the soles of your feet in the day that I shall do this, saith the LORD of hosts. (Malachi 4:1-3 KJV)

Paul also stated: "The wages of sin is death; but the gift of God is eternal life through Jesus Christ our Lord." (Romans 6:23 KJV)

And don't forget John 3:16, which I mentioned earlier. It features two opposites: perishing vs. everlasting life: "For God so loved the world that He gave His only begotten Son, that whoever believes in Him should not perish but have everlasting life." (NKJV)

So the Bible presents two clear potential destinies for all of us: eternal life or eternal death. It's as simple as that, and the choice is yours. Scripture clearly notes there is indeed eternal death for those who knowingly reject the truth of God. But God does not want us to be killed forever by being thrown into that lake of fire; He gets no thrill from it:

> As surely as I live, says the Sovereign LORD, I take no pleasure in the death of wicked people. I only want them to turn from their wicked ways so they can live. Turn! Turn from your wickedness ... (Ezekiel 33:11 NLT)

> I do not want anyone to die, says the Lord God, so change your hearts and lives so you may live. (Ezekiel 18:32 NCV)

It's amazing how the whole message of the Bible can sometimes be squeezed into a single verse or two, and those are two prime examples.

The God family is not hoping for Their own future children to be eternally dead despite their tendency to choose evil over good. They don't want anyone to die. They're begging people to stop their harmful ways so they can receive their extraordinary reward. Remember, the God family is having kids—the children of God.

Ask yourself this question: "Do I want my own kids to be dead forever?" Of course not. Well, your heavenly Father's not looking for that either. He wants everyone to choose His way of life and receive the gift of eternal life. And that's why there's something else coming that few people ever talk about: the second resurrection. Yes, there's more than one resurrection mentioned in Scripture. There's a first resurrection when Jesus returns, followed by a second resurrection that occurs a thousand years later. It's in your Bible, and we're going to look at it now, because it will lead to a fabulous truth that's rarely, if ever, discussed in most churches.

The Rest of the Dead

Once people rid themselves of the misconception about dying and immediately being alive in heaven, they'll see that among the final events mentioned in the New Testament are two separate resurrections from the dead. For all the truly obedient servants of God, there's "the first resurrection" that takes place, as we've seen, when Jesus comes back to Earth and is descending out of the sky. And then there's *another* major resurrection event later on. Here's how the Bible describes the sequence of events:

> Then I saw thrones, and the people sitting on them had been given the authority to judge. . . . They came to life again, and they reigned with Christ for a thousand years. This is the first resurrection. (The rest of the dead did not come back to life until the thousand years had ended.) Blessed and holy are those who share in the first resurrection. For them the second death holds no power, but they will be priests of God and of Christ and will reign with him a thousand years. (Revelation 20:4-6 NLT)

By now, you should be well-acquainted with this first resurrection. It's been discussed countless times in this book. It's the moment when faithful followers of Jesus through all time periods are quickened into their spirit-composed bodies to reveal themselves as the glorified, immortal children of God, and are given authority to judge and reign with Christ.

But the text continues with this all-important and often-overlooked verse: "The rest of the dead did not come back to life until the thousand years had ended." Once again, the Bible means what it says: The rest of the dead will come back to life *later*, after a millennium has gone by. The phrase "the rest of the dead" simply refers to everyone else who ever lived and did not get raised in the first resurrection upon the return of Jesus to Earth. This includes many who never heard the truth of God, and maybe others who were confused about it.

The Bible makes it clear that "as in Adam all die, even so in Christ ALL shall be made alive." (1 Corinthians 15:22 NKJV, emphasis added) As we've seen for many centuries, all human beings have died or are in the process of dying, including you and me. However, everyone who ever lived is coming back to life again by a resurrection from the dead. Your mom, your dad, all your siblings, children, ancestors, and distant relatives. Everyone else from all countries, all languages, all cultures, and through all time, from Adam and Eve onward. Even world famous celebrities such as Elvis Presley and Michael Jackson. They'll be back. If they're not quickened into immortal children of God during the first resurrection, they're going to be raised at the second resurrection, but with one major difference: It'll be only to a temporary, physical, flesh-and-blood existence—not an eternal life in a spirit-composed body.

Remember, only those in the first resurrection are immortal spirit beings, immune to the "second death," which is the eternal death: "Blessed and holy are those who share in the first resurrection. For them the second death holds no power." (v. 6) There's an obvious implication here: Because those in the first resurrection are immune from dying, those in the second resurrection, the so-called "rest of the dead," are not immune from death, and they could possibly be thrown into the lake of fire and killed. It's because they haven't been quickened into spirit bodies, but merely brought back to life in the physical bodies they originally had.

This was predicted in the book of Ezekiel when God said He'd take piles of dead bones and reanimate them with muscles, skin, and physical life:

> " 'This is what the Lord God says to the bones: I will cause breath to enter you so you will come to life. I will put muscles on you and flesh on you and cover you with skin. Then I will put breath in you so you will come to life. Then you will know that I am the Lord.' " (Ezekiel 37:5-6 NCV)

This grand event hasn't happened yet, but it will. "The rest of the dead" will include people from Israel as well as all other nations who never really knew that Jesus is the Lord, the Creator God of the Old Testament, the Word who existed with God the Father from time everlasting.

The sequence of events with the resurrected "rest of the dead" gets picked up later in the twentieth chapter of Revelation:

> And I saw a great white throne, and I saw the one who was sitting on it.... I saw the dead, both great and small, standing before God's throne. And the books were opened, including the Book of Life. And the dead were judged according to the things written in the books, according to what they had done. The sea gave up the dead in it, and death and the grave gave up the dead in them. They were all judged according to their deeds. (Revelation 20:12-13 NLT)

Here, the Bible describes all these formerly dead people coming out of their resting places, whether they were buried in the land or the sea, and they stand before God's throne, described as a great white throne. The dead who are brought back will even include people who had been devoured by sharks or vaporized by atomic blasts such as at Hiroshima and Nagasaki, Japan, during World War II. But even if their bodies had been completely destroyed previously, remember that they'll be returning to temporary life in physical, flesh-and-blood bodies once again.

The power of God is limitless, and those countless numbers of people will be restored to what they once looked like during their initial existence.

The text says the books were opened, referring to the books of the Bible and maybe even other books which have recorded the activities of their lives. It also mentions the Book of Life, which is apparently the book in which everyone raised in the second resurrection will want to have their names inscribed, because "anyone whose name was not found recorded in the Book of Life was thrown into the lake of fire." (v. 15 NLT)

Now here's where it gets especially intriguing. The Bible never actually says that every single one of these people standing before God's throne will unquestionably be tossed into the lake of fire and destroyed. As we just read, it specifically states that anyone whose name was not found recorded in the Book of Life was thrown into the lake of fire. Apparently, some people will be thrown into this lake of fire, but the wording is absolutely brilliant, because its slight vagueness suggests there's going to be a certain number of people—perhaps a whole bunch and maybe even the vast majority—who will NOT be tossed into that blazing furnace, because their names are indeed recorded (or will be recorded) in the Book of Life! Only those people whose names are not found in the Book of Life will go into the fire, and that could actually be very few when compared to the vast numbers of people who have lived since the time of the garden of Eden.

We know of at least three victims definitely going into the fire—the devil, the false prophet, and the beast—as Scripture indicates:

> The false prophet and the beast were thrown alive into the lake of fire that burns with sulfur. (Revelation 19:20 NCV)

> Then the devil, who had deceived them, was thrown into the fiery lake of burning sulfur, joining the beast and the false prophet. (Revelation 20:10 NLT)

Yet the text does not definitively specify anyone else by name. We've already seen a general outline of those whose fate is the second death:

> But the cowardly, the unbelieving, the vile, the murderers, the sexually immoral, those who practice magic arts, the idolaters and all liars— their place will be in the fiery lake of burning sulfur. This is the second death." (Revelation 21:8 NIV)

The Bible could have easily said that ALL those raised in the second resurrection, the great and the small standing before God, were thrown into the lake of fire. But it simply doesn't say that. Apparently, there will likely be at least some people brought back to temporary life during the second resurrection whose names will be included in the Book of Life!

The Bible specifically says, "The dead were judged according to the things written in the books, according to what they had done . . . They were all judged according to their deeds." This, my friends, is the time of judgment, or "Judgment Day," you've probably heard about at some point in your life. Human beings from across the globe and all time periods, not raised in the first resurrection to spirit life, will be raised a thousand years later in the second resurrection, back to physical life in order to be judged—in other words, to be tested and evaluated—but not automatically or universally condemned to eternal death.

It means people from the book of Genesis will be present, including citizens from the wicked cities of Sodom and Gomorrah. It means people throughout the Middle Ages who tortured and murdered believers for their faith in God will be there. It means

Adolf Hitler and his Nazi cohorts who slaughtered millions during World War II will be included. While some may indeed be headed for the lake of fire, I think many others will still have a chance to repent, to turn around and finally live God's way of life.

What I'm suggesting is that this time of final judgment is not necessarily a quick process, nor a definitively fatal event for everyone. I think all these billions of people will be raised to their physical, flesh-and-blood bodies again because God—who takes no pleasure in the death of the wicked—is going to give many of them an authentic chance to attain eternal life in the kingdom of God. I don't base this on conjecture, personal hunch, or whim. I'm going to show you numerous verses from the Bible supporting the contention that God will offer many people who did not make it in the first resurrection a real opportunity for salvation without any deception in the second resurrection, because He will exercise mercy on untold numbers of people who truly repent at that time.

Here Comes the Judgment

First, though, I'd like to dispel a common misconception about this final judgment. Many people picture this great-white-throne event as a trial-like scene with Jesus sitting in His judgment seat in a giant courtroom, and all those who have been raised to physical life walking toward Him, one by one, to hear the charges read against them. Then Jesus, after hearing all the deeds of a sinner's life, utters a very loud, "Guilty!" while slamming down a giant gavel. Perhaps there's an angel standing next to Jesus pulling the lever on a trap door, opening the floor for the person to plunge into some horrific abyss of the fatal lake of fire. Quite cinematic, yes, but found in the Bible? Not exactly.

What *is* found in Scripture is something far brighter, offering great hope and comfort to many. These people are indeed being raised to judgment, but it's important to keep in mind that a judgment is not a sentencing. It's merely a time of judging, a period of testing to evaluate a person's thoughts and actions, and that time period can sometimes be quite lengthy. For Christians today, their entire lifetime can be considered their day of judgment, and that's why true followers of Jesus are raised in the first resurrection, not having to wait for Round Two. God evaluates believers on a continuous basis, helping them become perfected and complete as they eventually reach their destination in the kingdom of God. So, perfected Christians have already been deemed worthy.

Here's a simple, interesting way to think about judgment, and it may help you understand where I'm going with this idea. When I use the word "judge" or "judgment," think of synonymous terms such as "testing" or "evaluation." With that in mind, you probably already know that right now in the United States and a few other countries, there are some very popular talent shows on television where participants sing, dance, or perform a skill in hopes of ultimately being crowned champion. You might recognize the names of some of these shows such as *American Idol* or *Dancing with the Stars*.

The final contestants on these programs are not facing some sort of quick, one-time "snap judgment." It doesn't take place in an instant. The hopefuls are viewed and *judged*—that is to say, *evaluated*—from week to week and given advice on how to better their talents and performance. They then practice throughout the following week to develop a higher level of skill for their singing or dancing, and perform once again for another time of *testing* and *evaluation*. The judgment cycle keeps repeating itself, and usually after a certain number of weeks, the contestants have grown and improved tremendously from their original state of readiness. In other words, the judging has helped to significantly better and perfect them, making them more complete. Then the winner gets to be crowned as champion.

This is analogous to what I believe is going to happen in the future when the second resurrection occurs. Although some unrepentant, wicked people are destined to be exterminated in the second death, many of the people who never heard or understood God's secret plan during their human lifetimes will finally have it clearly explained to them after they've been raised back to their temporary, physical lives. Yes, they'll find out they're guilty, of course, because we're all guilty of having violated at least some of God's laws:

> As the Scriptures say: "There is no one who always does what is right, not even one." (Romans 3:10 NCV)

> Everyone has sinned and fallen short of God's glorious standard. (Romans 3:23 NCV)

But they'll also learn the very Good News, that their eternal death penalty has already been paid by Jesus, and they can be forgiven of their sins if they truly turn toward God's instructions. They'll then be given a certain amount of time to admit they've been following the wrong path and to change their way of life so as to follow the ways of their Creator. Just like true Christians do today, these people can then improve themselves through trials and testing to develop their godly character, finally learning how to subdue, overcome, and master the sinful nature embedded in their minds from their original lifetimes' worth of satanically inspired brainwashing and confusion. Ultimately, these people, too, can be perfected and crowned with the same glory Jesus received, just like those who received the sensational reward in the first resurrection.

In various places in both the Old and New Testaments, Jesus discussed the judging cycle for "the rest of the dead" who will have been brought back to temporary life in the second resurrection. He made it clear that during His short lifetime on Earth, He was

NOT judging (or evaluating) the world, especially those who did not believe His teaching:

> "Anyone who hears my words and does not obey them, I do not judge, because I did not come to judge the world, but to save the world. There is a judge for those who refuse to believe in me and do not accept my words. The word I have taught will be their judge on the last day." (John 12:47-48 NCV)

Feel free to read those verses over again, and let the remarkable truth sink in. Out of His own mouth, Jesus said He was not judging those people who heard His words and chose not to obey them in their initial lifetimes. Their judgment—that is to say, their ultimate evaluation—will be in the future, *on the last day*, the time of the second resurrection, when they will be judged. God's timeless instruction, the sacred word He taught, is the standard by which they'll be evaluated. Many of these people will apparently have a chance to repent and to get with the glorious program. And, yes, it'll be Jesus, in fact, acting as the top Judge of the future:

> But the Lord reigns forever, executing judgment from his throne. He will judge the world with justice and rule the nations with fairness. (Psalm 9:7-8 NLT)

> "In fact, the Father judges no one, but he has given the Son power to do all the judging . . ." (John 5:22 NCV)

Speaking of this future period of learning and testing, Jesus said many formerly disobedient people would actually have a new willingness to accept God's truth instead of being so averse or even hostile to it:

"People who do wrong will now understand. Those who complain will accept being taught." (Isaiah 29:24 NCV)

I will teach all your children, and they will enjoy great peace. (Isaiah 54:13 NLT)

As it is written in the Scriptures, 'They will all be taught by God.' (John 6:45 NLT)

Indeed, Jesus will be personally teaching people after His return, and He won't do it all by Himself. At least some of the instruction will come from the formerly human and freshly divine members of the family of God. Remember, the quickened believers from the first resurrection will be monitoring and helping as judges, because, as we've read, they "had been given the authority to judge." (Revelation 20:4 NLT)

The Bible says they're the judges. They're the testers. They're the evaluators. They're the teachers. The children of God are going to be the shepherds and coaches of the future, examining, evaluating, and judging the daily activities of many who never heard the magnificent message or who never truly and earnestly submitted to it in their original lives due to deception, distraction, or confusion. The goal is to help as many as possible repent and reach eternal life as well. Jesus explained it'll involve a constant monitoring of individuals, not from a God or angels they never see, but from teachers who will often make themselves visible:

> . . . your teachers will be hidden no more; with your own eyes you will see them. Whether you turn to the right or to the left, your ears will hear a voice behind you, saying, "This is the way; walk in it." (Isaiah 30:20-21 NIV)

> And I will give you shepherds after my own
> heart, who will guide you with knowledge and
> understanding . . . In that day Jerusalem will be
> known as 'The Throne of the LORD.' All nations
> will come there to honor the LORD. They will no
> longer stubbornly follow their own evil desires.
> (Jeremiah 3:15-17 NLT)

This is all truly important. Many people today are under the
mistaken impression that if someone never hears the message of
God or never responds to the truth, there's no hope for that person,
and he or she is completely done for. Thankfully, the Bible seems
to teach differently, as those who get raised to immortality during
the first resurrection will be leaders and guides for many others.
It's because their character will have already been perfected, and
they will know how to overcome the evil and choose the good. In
case you never noticed it before, Jesus in both the Old and New
Testaments instructed his followers to make proper judgments
(evaluations) about virtually everything, to help prepare them for
this judgment time in the future!

> These are the things that ye shall do; Speak ye every
> man the truth to his neighbour; EXECUTE THE
> JUDGMENT OF TRUTH AND PEACE in your
> gates . . . (Zechariah 8:16 KJV, emphasis added)

> "Do not judge according to appearance, but judge
> with righteous judgment." (John 7:24 NKJV)

And remember what we've already seen from Paul, who
makes it glaringly obvious that our judgment calls during our
initial, physical lifetime help qualify and prepare us to be expert
judges in our spirit-composed, eternal lifetime:

> Surely you know that God's people will judge the
> world. So if you are to judge the world, are you not
> able to judge small cases as well? You know that in

the future we will judge angels, so surely we can judge the ordinary things of this life. (1 Corinthians 6:2-3 NCV)

Now, precisely how long will "the rest of the dead" who come back to life get to spend in their resurrected physical bodies for this time of instruction and coaching by the children of God? I can't say for sure, but the Bible in one place hints at a lifespan of one hundred years.

We actually saw this quote earlier as part of the future paradise conditions mentioned by God in Isaiah, but I didn't focus on this verse:

"No more shall an infant from there live but a few days, Nor an old man who has not fulfilled his days; For the child shall die one hundred years old, But the sinner being one hundred years old shall be accursed. (Isaiah 65:20 NKJV)

Why might Scripture suggest that the children of the future will get a hundred-year lifespan and that sinners at the century mark shall be accursed? Possibly because this will be the amount of time granted for that future time of judgment and testing for people to finally turn to God. They may get a hundred years of temporary existence to once again go through life, but this time clearly knowing the truth about God, the divine rules, and the ultimate glorious destiny that's meant for them. They may then be guided by people who have already overcome the ways of the world, the ways that lead to death, and who have already been made immortal. If the people raised in the second resurrection still refuse to repent, their only other option is eternal death in the lake of fire. That could be what's referred to by "the sinner being one hundred years old shall be accursed."

And will most people repent and finally accept God? I strongly suspect they will, and here's why. Jesus promised in the

Old Testament: "I have sworn by my own name, and I will never go back on my word: Every knee will bow to me, and every tongue will confess allegiance to my name." (Isaiah 45:23 NLT) The New Century Version of this same quote translates the last portion as "I promise that everyone will bow before me and will promise to follow me."

In this quotation, Jesus sounded like he meant business, because He swore by His own name and indicated no backpedaling. He said every knee will bow to Him and every tongue will confess allegiance to His name, or promise to follow Him, depending on the translation. If the Bible means what it says—and it does, of course—then we should expect a massive repentance of millions or billions of people away from the carnal mind, away from a sinful nature, and a return to God after the second resurrection takes place.

Jesus' promise was reiterated in the New Testament by Paul, who added an extra piece of information that adds more support to this scenario:

> "Therefore God also has highly exalted Him and given Him the name which is above every name, that at the name of Jesus every knee should bow, of those in heaven, and of those on earth, and of THOSE UNDER THE EARTH, and that every tongue should confess that Jesus Christ is Lord, to the glory of God the Father." (Philippians 2:9-11 NKJV, emphasis added)

Paul specifically mentioned "those under the earth" as being among those whose knees will bow and whose tongues will confess that Jesus Christ is Lord. He was referring to the countless number of people still in their graves, as well as the billions of others who will have died by the time Jesus returns to Earth. Paul explained that they'd eventually be bowing to Jesus in allegiance after they're brought back to life in the second resurrection.

A good indicator of future hope for nonbelievers came from the mouth of Jesus, as He dispatched his followers to preach the good news of the kingdom of God in many towns. But knowing that some people who heard His message would not accept the truth, He stated:

> If any household or town refuses to welcome you or listen to your message, shake its dust from your feet as you leave. I tell you the truth, the wicked cities of Sodom and Gomorrah will be better off than such a town on the judgment day. (Matthew 10:14-15 NLT)

This is intriguing, because the citizens of Sodom and Gomorrah were firebombed to death by Jesus Himself thousands of years ago in the nineteenth chapter of Genesis because of the inhabitants' wicked, ungodly behavior. Yet Jesus indicated that on Judgment Day, those perverted sinners would actually be better off than other people who heard the message of God and refused to respond to it. Why? Because the folks in Sodom and Gomorrah never really had the truth proclaimed to them, so they did not have a true opportunity to respond and follow God. In other words, they'll be better off because, despite their previous wickedness, they may still have a chance to repent on Judgment Day, while those who have already heard God's message and rejected it outright might not have that chance.

Here's another eye-opening account from the New Testament that bolsters what I'm saying, and this is rarely dealt with in church sermons because it goes against what so many people wrongly assume about the future. It involves Paul finding out about a Christian man engaged in a serious sin—having sex with his stepmother:

> I can hardly believe the report about the sexual immorality going on among you, something so evil that even the pagans don't do it. I am told that you have a man in your church who is living in sin with his father's wife. And you are so proud of yourselves! Why aren't you mourning in sorrow and shame? And why haven't you removed this man from your fellowship? Even though I am not there with you in person, I am with you in the Spirit. Concerning the one who has done this, I have already passed judgment in the name of the Lord Jesus. You are to call a meeting of the church, and I will be there in spirit, and the power of the Lord Jesus will be with you as you meet. Then you must cast this man out of the church and into Satan's hands, so that his sinful nature will be destroyed and he himself will be saved when the Lord returns. (1 Corinthians 5:1-5 NLT)

This is an interesting account because a typical Christian church today would most likely take a very different approach than Paul, thinking that it had to do whatever it could to stop this man from sinning now in this life and rescue him from the eternal punishment of death. But Paul said to do the exact opposite. He instructed the church at Corinth to immediately expel this clown from their group and let him fall into the hands of Satan the devil! In case you're not understanding the significance, he did *not* say to keep this man in the hands of Jesus to rescue him now! The Christian apostle Paul ordered a Christian congregation to kick out a Christian man and turn him over to the enemy known as Satan. He didn't even try to convince the church members to encourage this man to repent of his sin.

And why, according to Paul, was that the correct course of action? "So that his sinful nature will be destroyed and he himself will be saved when the Lord returns." As I'm trying to get across, Paul seems to indicate there will likely be a future opportunity for many people who didn't receive the reward in the first resurrection to repent later, after the second resurrection, and still be saved once their sinful human nature is eventually destroyed! It's simply sublime. However, for those who might be thinking a future chance at salvation is a license to continue sinning in their current life, Paul also warned:

> Well then, since God's grace has set us free from the law, does that mean we can go on sinning? Of course not! (Romans 6:15 NLT)

Amazing Patience

Continuing now with the future, Jesus Himself indicated He came to Earth so He could save the lost, and He and His Father are not looking to lose anyone:

> For the Son of man is come to seek and to save that which was lost. (Luke 19:10 KJV)

> If a man owns a hundred sheep, and one of them wanders away, will he not leave the ninety-nine on the hills and go to look for the one that wandered off? And if he finds it, truly I tell you, he is happier about that one sheep than about the ninety-nine that did not wander off. In the same way your Father in heaven is not willing that any of these little ones should perish. (Matthew 18:12-14 NIV)

When it comes to repentance and ultimate salvation, it appears we're just not dealing with a now-or-never situation. Our timetable is not God's timetable. The God family will save people whenever They want to save people, and apparently God is taking plenty of time, saving people in different time periods—

some now, and others later. God is obviously showing abundant patience with us, and Paul used himself to demonstrate that patience. Paul called himself chief of the sinners, the worst kind there is, but said he was being used as an example to show how God is not working the divine plan in some rushed time frame:

> What I say is true, and you should fully accept it: Christ Jesus came into the world to save sinners, of whom I am the worst. But I was given mercy so that in me, the worst of all sinners, Christ Jesus could show that he has patience without limit. His patience with me made me an example for those who would believe in him and have life forever. (1 Timothy 1:15-16 NCV)

And Peter concisely summed up the reason God has been taking plenty of time:

> The Lord isn't really being slow about his promise, as some people think. No, he is being patient for your sake. He does not want anyone to be destroyed, but wants everyone to repent. (2 Peter 3:9 NLT)

God's patience is indeed without limit, and God wants everyone to knock it off, to stop being disobedient. This is why I think many people will get a real, unhindered chance at salvation in the second resurrection. Over and over again, the Bible describes God as one whose mercy endures forever. In fact, that exact phrase, "mercy endures forever," is found a whopping forty-one times in the New King James translation. A typical example is, "Oh, give thanks to the God of gods! For His mercy endures forever." (Psalm 136:2 NKJV) Because His mercy endures forever, then won't it continue during the time of the second resurrection? Won't God then accept truly heartbroken people finally looking to embrace Him once their eyes are opened to the truth and they see Him in all His glory? I think He will. In light of that, consider this famous question about forgiveness that Peter asked of Jesus:

> Then Peter came to him and asked, "Lord, how often should I forgive someone who sins against me? Seven times?" "No!" Jesus replied, "seventy times seven!" (Matthew 18:21-22 NLT)

Clearly, this is an instruction from Jesus that we're supposed to keep forgiving people over and over again. Now think about this for a moment. Is God teaching us human beings to repeatedly forgive people for their sins, yet God won't do the same for those who never even heard the name of Jesus Christ in their lifetime? Is God going to toss these people into a lake of fire even though they never had the chance in their lives to repent? God, of course, will be the ultimate Judge about that, but I honestly think He will be merciful toward them.

Scripture does not portray God as being unfair, but says, "He is the Rock; his work is perfect. Everything he does is just and fair. He is a faithful God who does no wrong; how just and upright he is!" (Deuteronomy 32:4 NLT)

If God does not forgive repenter-wannabes in the second resurrection and merely condemns them to eternal death, would that make us human beings more merciful than our Creator, whose mercy is said to endure forever, because we continually forgive people and God doesn't? My point is: God has more mercy than we can possibly fathom, and I believe there will be a time of forgiveness and salvation in the future for many people who repent.

I understand this concept may seem very new, strange, and even somewhat mysterious to you. Well, it is a mystery, and the Bible itself calls it a mystery, because it's all part of the divine secret that so many people have never quite figured out. In the eleventh chapter of Romans, Paul did his best to unravel this puzzle for some formerly pagan people who became believers. He wanted them to know that even Jews and others who failed to embrace the truth of God might still have the opportunity to be saved in the future:

> I want you to understand this mystery, dear brothers and sisters, so that you will not feel proud and start bragging. Some of the Jews have hard hearts, but this will last only until the complete number of Gentiles comes to Christ. And so all Israel will be saved. Do you remember what the prophets said about this? "A Deliverer will come from Jerusalem, and he will turn Israel from all ungodliness. And then I will keep my covenant with them and take away their sins."
>
> Many of the Jews are now enemies of the Good News. But this has been to your benefit, for God has given his gifts to you Gentiles. Yet the Jews are still his chosen people because of his promises to Abraham, Isaac, and Jacob. For God's gifts and his call can never be withdrawn. Once, you Gentiles were rebels against God, but when the Jews refused his mercy, God was merciful to you instead.
>
> And now, in the same way, the Jews are the rebels, and God's mercy has come to you. But someday they, too, will share in God's mercy. For God has imprisoned all people in their own disobedience so he could have mercy on everyone. Oh, what a wonderful God we have! How great are his riches and wisdom and knowledge! How impossible it is for us to understand his decisions and his methods! (Romans 11:25-33 NLT)

These nine verses of Scripture need to be highlighted in everyone's Bible and read numerous times, because they provide an uplifting answer to the nagging question about what happens to everyone else who didn't believe in, or never were exposed to, God's message. Paul noted that despite the fact that many Jews were then enemies of God's message, ALL ISRAEL WILL BE SAVED. Those are the words on the page. He said God will keep His covenant with them and take away their sins.

He continued: "And now, in the same way, the Jews are the rebels, and God's mercy has come to you. But someday they, too, will share in God's mercy. For God has imprisoned all people in their own disobedience so he could have mercy on everyone." (vv. 31-32)

Yes, the Bible says Jesus-rejecting Jews are the rebels right now, but they're going to share in God's mercy someday in the future. That'll be after the second resurrection. Paul also declared that GOD is actually imprisoning ALL people in their own disobedience. Why? So MERCY CAN BE GIVEN TO EVERYONE in the future! God really does wish to save everyone from all tribes and nations, and will likely provide them the opportunity to repent and obey later on.

It's a fantastic, mind-quaking plan of salvation, to make sure people have a very real chance to finally gain eternal life in the kingdom. Even Paul marveled at its magnitude, saying, "Oh, what a wonderful God we have! How great are his riches and wisdom and knowledge! How impossible it is for us to understand his decisions and his methods!" (v. 33)

The conclusion is inescapable that, during the time in which we live, God is a great concealer. The divine family is intentionally not saving everyone at this time, but apparently will give many people a chance at salvation later: As the Scriptures say:

"God has put them into a deep sleep. To this very day he has shut their eyes so they do not see, and closed their ears so they do not hear." (Romans 11:8 NLT)

I know it surprises people, but God is, in fact, intentionally preventing most people from understanding the truth in this present evil age. Jesus Himself said it's *impossible* for people to come to Him unless they're specifically being called by God the Father:

For no one can come to me unless the Father who sent me draws them to me ... (John 6:44 NLT)

And yet shortly before He was put to death, Jesus said:

And when I am lifted up from the earth, I will draw EVERYONE to myself. (John 12:32 NLT, emphasis added)

Obviously, this prediction has not been fulfilled yet, because everyone is not being drawn to Jesus right now. But He said they *will be* drawn to Him in the future, when there's no more concealing of the message!

Remember what we saw in the early part of this book—that Jesus intentionally spoke in puzzling parables. He taught that He was hiding His message from most people on purpose, intending it only for a select few at the time:

You are permitted to understand the secret about the Kingdom of God. But I am using these stories to conceal everything about it from outsiders . . . (Mark 4:11 NLT)

To you it has been given to know the mysteries of the kingdom of God, but to the rest it is given in parables, that 'Seeing they may not see, And hearing they may not understand.' (Luke 8:10 NKJV)

Because it has been given to you to know the mysteries of the kingdom of heaven, but to them it has not been given. (Matthew 13:11 NKJV)

The truth about the mysteries of the kingdom of God—the divine secret, as I call it—is simply not meant for everyone to fully grasp during this age, but is available now for those who truly desire it and seek it. It'll be made fully available to others when the God family comes to Earth with huge numbers of brand-new members to help educate those never exposed to it or who never understood it. The consummate birth of human beings into the God family will take place on God's schedule, not ours. It will happen during a time when Satan the devil, who is called the "god of this world" or "god of this age" (2 Corinthians 4:4), has been taken out of the picture, having been tossed into the lake of fire, and people are finally able to learn the truth without the clever deception that now covers the world.

Only then will most people ultimately understand who their Creator really is—that He's Yeshua, Jesus of Nazareth, the member of the God family who has existed since time immemorial, who left the unseen dimension of heaven to live with and save His own creation so they could join Him as the literal children of God in God's immortal family. People will see some of their fellow former human beings, who have undergone a glorious metamorphosis and been transformed into radiant, spirit-composed bodies, helping to administer God's very own government here on Planet Earth and potentially throughout the rest of the universe.

Yes, Scripture teaches us that the rest of the universe is anxiously anticipating the moment when God's children will be revealed in their full glory:

> For all creation is waiting eagerly for that future day when God will reveal who his children really are. Against its will, everything on earth was subjected to God's curse. All creation anticipates the day when it will join God's children in glorious freedom from death and decay. For we know that all creation has been groaning as in the pains of childbirth right up to the present time. And even we Christians, although we have the Holy Spirit within us as a foretaste of future glory, also groan to be released from pain and suffering. We, too, wait anxiously for that day when God will give us our full rights as his children, including the new bodies he has promised us. (Romans 8:19-23 NLT)

If you ever wondered why the universe is filled with billions of galaxies, each with untold billions of stars and countless numbers of dead planets, it may very well be because the divine family of God is meant to get incredibly large and expand into the vast domain of deep space. We're told that "All creation anticipates the day when it will join God's children in glorious but freedom from death and decay." So not only are human beings meant to be transformed into something glorious, but all those lifeless planets that dwell in the farthest reaches of the universe will apparently be freed from their state of lifelessness as well. The divine children of God are meant to inherit and have authority over "all things," and the universe is the epitome of "all things."

The future is far more phenomenal than what most people have been led to believe. The divine secret is that, if we change our disobedient ways, become obedient to Jesus, and allow Christ to live in us so we can overcome our sinful human nature, everyone can become divine and be born into the actual family of God who created us thousands of years ago. Through challenges and suffering, we as human beings can be perfected and become complete, learning and developing the very character that God the Father and Jesus the Christ already possess. All of us, therefore, have the tremendous opportunity to be quickened by the Spirit of God that dwells in us to be changed into the glorious, immortal children of God.

In the final book of the Bible, just look what Jesus Christ has promised for everyone who overcomes:

> To him who overcomes I will give to eat from the tree of life, which is in the midst of the Paradise of God. (Revelation 2:7 NKJV)

> He who overcomes shall not be hurt by the second death. (2:11)

> To him who overcomes I will give some of the hidden manna to eat. And I will give him a white stone, and on the stone a new name written which no one knows except him who receives it. (2:17)

> And he who overcomes, and keeps My works until the end, to him I will give power over the nations— 'He shall rule them with a rod of iron ...' (2:26-27)

> He who overcomes shall be clothed in white garments, and I will not blot out his name from the Book of Life; but I will confess his name before My Father and before His angels. (3:5)

> He who overcomes, I will make him a pillar in the temple of My God, and he shall go out no more. I will write on him the name of My God and the name of the city of My God, the New Jerusalem, which comes down out of heaven from My God. And I will write on him My new name. (3:12)

> To him who overcomes I will grant to sit with Me on My throne, as I also overcame and sat down with My Father on His throne. (3:21)

> He who overcomes shall inherit all things, and I will be his God and he shall be My son. (21:7)

This is your intended, glorious future. Repent and overcome to be part of the first resurrection, and finally set your mind at ease. Embrace your precious, awesome destiny as a divine child of God.

Subject Index

Abednego, 96–100
Abel, 135
Abraham, 83–85, 91, 133, 135
Adam
  creation of, 28–29, 53
  earthly body of, 62–63, 67
  eats from tree of knowledge of good
    and evil, 89
  Eve created from, 54
afterlife. See quickening from mortal to
immortal
angels
  at the birth of Jesus, 92
  judged/ruled over by us, 135–37
  kingdom of, 125
  at the Resurrection, 92–93
  role of, 130
  Second Coming forecast by, 107
  visibility and invisibility of, 91–94
apostles, 134. See also Paul

Barnabas, 147
beast, 160
Bible. See also the Scripture Index
  casual reading, 5
  illiteracy, 3
  secret revealed (see divine secret)
  source of truth, 1–2, 11
Book of Life, 159–60

Cain, 145–46, 152
character development (training for
godliness), 142–47, 151
Christ. See Jesus Christ
Crucifixion, 12–13, 26

Daniel, 14–15
David, King, 127, 133–34, 135
death, eternal (perishing), 50, 154–56,
157–61
Destination Unknown (Missing Persons),
4
devil (Satan), 160, 177
divine secret, 9–47
  Bible quotations mentioning, 12–14
  children of God, 31–40, 42–43, 46–47
  defined, 10–11

God as family in Heaven, 23–26, 37
  (see also God, children of; kingdom
  of God)
  human beings becoming divine/
  immortal, 40–47 (see also quickening
  from mortal to immortal)
  human beings made in God's image,
  26–32
  importance/scope, 10
  life forms made in their own image/
  after their own kind, 27–30
  overview, 9–14
  reason for hiding it, 13–14, 176–77
  reason for revealing it, 32
  revealed, 14–17, 31–32, 75–76, 178–79
  and the Second Coming, 35–36 (see
  also Second Coming)
  "secret" defined, 10
  the Word in the real beginning, 17–23

Earth
  kingdom of God on, 105, 108–10
  renewal of, 110–23
Eden, 88–89
Elohim, 18–19, 26, 42, 125
enemies, love of, 152–53
Enoch, 135
eternal death (perishing), 50, 154–61
eternal life, 41, 154–56. See also
quickening from mortal to immortal
Eve, 54, 89

false prophet, 160
Feast of Tabernacles, 87–88, 109

God
  children of, 31–40, 42–43, 46–47
  as family in Heaven, 23–26, 37 (see
  also God, children of; kingdom of
  God)
  as Father vs. Jesus, 22–23
  human beings created in Their image,
  26–29
  as Jesus, 20–22
  knowledge/wisdom of, 90
  life forms created, 27–30
  obedience to, 149–50, 154, 165

physical attributes, 29–30
as plural, 18–19, 26
as spirit, 18
translated from Hebrew Elohim,
18–19, 26, 42, 125
visibility and invisibility of, 91
as the Word, 18–20

heavenly bodies, 65. See also stars
human beings
becoming divine/immortal, 40–47
created from dirt, 28–29
Jesus' power to quicken, 67–68
kingdom of God ruled by, 130–40
made in God's image, 26–32
miraculous/supernatural feats by,
95–102
perception of miracles, 101–2
sinful nature, 142, 145–46, 163–64,
170–71 (see also kingdom of God,
training for godliness)
understanding/knowledge, 90

immortality. See quickening from mortal
to immortal
invisibility and visibility, 91–95
Isaac, 133, 135
Israelites, 80–81, 88, 134, 148–49

Jacob, 133, 135
Jesus Christ. See also Second Coming
advising Cain, 145–46
on being the Christ/Messiah/Savior,
43–44
birth, 3, 92, 126–27
bowing/allegiance to, 168–69
before creation, 23
Crucifixion, 12–13, 26
dining with Abraham, 83–85, 91
eating and drinking by, 86–88
on evildoers as hating the light, 73
on forgiveness for sins, 173
furnace miracle, 96–100
glorified by God, 37–38, 55
God as, 20–22
on God's laws, 134
on hope for nonbelievers, 169
"Jesus" translated from Hebrew
Yeshua, 23
Jews' stoning of, 43–44

judgment by, 164–65
kingdom of God ruled by, 118, 127–30
landing on Mount of Olives, 106–8
Last Supper, 87
and Nicodemus, 57–61, 94
parables/stories used, 13–14, 137–40,
176–77
prayer before execution, 25
Resurrection, 36, 92–93
on secrets/mysteries, 13–15
servants of, 13
shining body of, 78–79, 81
suffering of, 147–48, 151
Transfiguration, 81
visibility and invisibility of, 91
vs. God as Father, 22–23
water changed to wine by, 95–96
as the Word/Creator, 20–22, 39, 44
Jews, 174–75. See also Israelites
Joseph, 135
Judgment Day, 160–71

kingdom of God, 103–80
animals in, 114–16
brought to Earth (see quickening from
mortal to immortal; Second Coming)
defined, 125
on Earth, 105, 108–10
Earth's renewal, 110–23
God's laws in, 134
God's patience for saving the lost,
171–80
hope for nonbelievers, 153–56, 169
Jesus' landing on Mount of Olives,
106–8
Judgment Day, 160–71
"kingdom" defined, 124–25
meaning of life, 140–53
New Jerusalem brought by God the
Father, 118–21, 135
overview, 103–10
people we'll see in, 133–35
resurrection of dead faithful followers,
156–57
resurrection of other dead, 156–61,
163, 172
ruled by Jesus, 118, 127–30
ruled by us, 130–40
and the Second Coming, 105–6
training for godliness (character

development), 142–47, 151
and the universe, 177–78
and the well-being of others,
151–52
when it starts, 138–39
knowledge, 89–90
Kovacs, Joe, 1–2
Shocked by the Bible, 2–4

lake of fire. See eternal death
Last Supper, 87
life. See also questions about life
eternal (life after death), 41,
154–56 (see also quickening from
mortal to immortal)
meaning of, 4, 140–53
tree of, 88–89
life forms made in their own image/
after their own kind, 27–30
loving others, 152–53

manna, 88, 179
mansions, 122
meaning of life, 4, 140–53
mercy, 172–74
Meshach, 96–100
miracles
after quickening, 95–102
furnace story, 96–100
human perception of, 101–2
water changed to wine by Jesus,
95–96
Missing Persons: Destination
Unknown, 4
Moses, 80–81, 91, 135
Mount of Olives, 106–8

Nebuchadnezzar, King, 14–15, 96–99
New Jerusalem, 118–21, 135
New Testament. See specific books in
the Scripture Index
Nicodemus, 57–61, 94
Noah, 135
Noah's ark, 3
nonbelievers, hope for, 153–56, 169

Old Testament. See specific books in
the Scripture Index; specific books in
the Scripture Index

Paul
on the Crucifixion, 12–13
on eternal life, 41
on glorification of God's children,
39
on God as Father vs. Jesus, 22
on God's knowledge/wisdom, 90
on God's laws, 134
on hidden/revealed secrets, 12–13,
16, 31–32, 46–47, 69
on human understanding/
knowledge, 90
on Jesus as Creator, 21
on Jews, 174–75
on judgment by people, 167
on physical vs. spiritual bodies,
68–69
on the quickening, 71, 74
on repentance, 168–69
seed analogy, 64
on sin, 146, 154, 170–71, 172
on stars, 65
on suffering's purpose, 146–47
peace, 117–18
perishing (eternal death), 50, 154–61
Pharisees, 58
Pilate, Pontius, 128
prayers, 114

questions about life
What happens to people who
haven't heard God's message or
don't believe? 4, 153–56, 169
What is God doing with people? 4,
141, 148–49
What is the meaning of life? 4,
140–53
What will happen when Jesus
returns? 4 (see also kingdom of
God; quickening from mortal to
immortal; Second Coming)
Why are we here? 4, 140
quickening from mortal to immortal,
49–102
angels at, 74–76
bodily ingredients for, 53–56
born (again) of spirit, 56–61,
66–69
the changing, 49–52, 61–69
of the dead, then the living, 73–74,

76
defined, 50–51
eating and
drinking after,
82–89
events signaling,
72
Jesus' power
to quicken us,
67–68
knowledge and
powers following,
89–90
miraculous/
supernatural
feats, 95–102
overview, 49–53
resurrection of
the dead, 62,
65–66, 70
at the Second
Coming, 69–76
seed analogy,
64–66
shining bodies,
77–82
sinless existence,
76–77
trumpet
signaling, 63, 69,
71–76
visibility and
invisibility, 91–95

rebirth. See
quickening from
mortal to immortal,
born (again) of
spirit
repentance, 153–55,
161, 167–69, 172,
179–80
resurrection
of dead faithful
followers, 156–57
of Jesus, 36,
92–93
of other dead,
156–61, 163, 172
and quickening,
62, 65–66, 70

salvation. See eternal
life; repentance;
resurrection
Samson, 135
Sarah, 135
Satan (devil), 160,
177
Scripture. See Bible
and the Scripture
Index
Second Coming.
See also kingdom
of God
and the divine
secret, 35–36
Feast of
Tabernacles
following, 87–88
Jesus' landing on
Mount of Olives,
106–8
mourning about,
72–73
predicted, 128
quickening at,
69–76
trumpet
signaling, 63, 69,
71–76
secret revealed in
the Bible, 1, 6. See
also divine secret
Shadrach, 96–100
shining bodies after
quickening, 77–82
Shocked by the Bible
(Kovacs), 2–4
sin
defined, 77
forgiveness for,
173
our sinful nature,
142, 145–46, 163–
64, 170–71 (see
also kingdom of
God, training for
godliness)
sexual
immorality, 170
sinless existence
after quickening,

76–77
Sodom and
Gomorrah, 169
Solomon, King, 143
stars, 65, 72, 178
Stephen, 81
suffering and
tribulations, 72, 143,
146–48, 150–51

Ten
Commandments,
77, 80–81
Theos, 125. See also
Elohim
training for
godliness (character
development), 142–
47, 151
Transfiguration, 81
tree of knowledge of
good and evil, 89
tree of life, 88–89
tribulations. See
suffering and
tribulations
trumpet signaling
quickening, 63, 69,
71–76
truth, Bible as
source of, 1–2, 11

universe, 177–78

visibility and
invisibility, 91–95

wind and spirit, 94
wise men at the
birth of Jesus, 3, 127
the Word
Jesus as, 20–22,
39, 44
in the real
beginning, 17–23

Yeshua, 23. See also
Jesus Christ

Scripture Index

Acts
1:11 NKJV, 36
1:11–12 NCV, 107
6:15 NLT, 81
7:28–29 NKJV, 33
7:55 NLT, 30
10:41 NCV, 86
14:22 NCV, 147
Amos
3:7 NKJV, 15

Colossians
1:16 NKJV, 21
1:25–27 NLT, 31–32
1:26 NCV, 12, 16
1:27 NLT, 39
3:1 NKJV, 30
3:4 NCV, 38
1 Corinthians
2:7 NKJV, 12
2:7–8 NCV, 39
2:7–10 NLT, 47
2:8 NCV, 12–13
5:1–5 NLT, 170
6:2–3 NCV, 167
6:2–3 NLT, 136
13:12 NLT, 90
15:6 NKJV, 157
15:22 NKJV, 157
15:22–23 NLT, 70
15:28 NLT, 42
15:35–53 NLT, 61–63
15:36–38 NLT, 64
15:39–41 NLT, 65
15:42–44 NLT, 65–66
15:45 KJV, 53
15:45 NLT, 67
15:46–49 NLT, 68

15:48 NLT, 78
15:50 KJV, 69
15:50 NCV, 56
15:50 NIV, 69
15:50 NKJV, 56, 69
15:50 NLT, 56, 68
15:51 NKJV, 49
15:51–53 NLT, 69
15:52 NLT, 75
15:53 NKJV, 51
2 Corinthians
4:4, 177
4:17 NCV, 38
4:17–18 NLT, 151
6:18 NCV, 34
7:1 NIV, 146

Daniel
2:21–22 NKJV, 14
2:28 NKJV, 15
2:47 NKJV, 15
3:4–6 NCV, 96–97
3:12 NCV, 97
3:15 NCV, 97
3:16–18 NCV, 97–98
3:19–23 NCV, 98
3:24–25 NCV, 99
3:26–27 NCV, 99
7:18 NCV, 132
7:27 NCV, 132
12:2–3 NLT, 79
12:4 KJV, 32
Deuteronomy
5:29 NCV, 142–43
8:2 NCV, 148–49
16:13–15 NKJV, 88
30:19–20 NLT, 144
32:4 NLT, 173

Ecclesiastes
12:13 KJV, 143
Ephesians
1:18 NKJV, 39
2:8, 147
2:10 NLT, 141
3:3–6 NLT, 46
3:9 NKJV, 21
3:9 NLT, 16
3:14–15 NKJV, 24, 37
3:19 NKJV, 41
6:19 NCV, 16
Exodus
16:31 NKJV, 88
31:18 NKJV, 30
34:29–35 NIV, 80–81
Ezekiel
1:27–28 NLT, 78–79
18:32 NCV, 155
33:11 NLT, 155
36:33–38 NLT, 113
37:5–6 NCV, 158
37:24–25 NCV, 133–34
37:26–28 KJV, 106

Galatians
1:1 NCV, 22
3:26 NKJV, 34
Genesis
1:1 NKJV, 17
1:11–12 NKJV, 27
1:21 NKJV, 27
1:24–25 NKJV, 27
1:26 KJV, 26
1:26 NCV, 26, 133
1:26 NIV, 26
1:26 NKJV, 26

1:26 NLT, 26
2:7 NCV, 28
2:21–23 NKJV, 54
3:6, 89
4:6–7 NCV, 145–46
4:9 NKJV, 152
8:4, 3
18:1–8 NLT, 83–84

Habakkuk
3:4 NCV, 78
Hebrews
1:8 NCV, 23
1:14 NCV, 130
2:5 NCV, 129
2:6–8 NLT, 136
2:10 NCV, 38, 147
2:10 NKJV, 38
2:11–13 NCV, 36–37
5:8–9 NKJV, 147
11:10 NCV, 135
11:13 NCV, 135
11:16 NCV, 135
13:2 NCV, 93

Isaiah
2:2–3 NKJV, 108–9
2:4 NLT, 117
9:6–7 NKJV, 126
11:6–9 NCV, 115–16
29:24 NCV, 165
30:20–21 NIV, 166
35 NCV, 111–12
40:4 NCV, 117
40:5 NKJV, 30
40:10 NLT, 127
44:24 NIV, 22
45:12 NCV, 30
45:23 NCV, 168
45:23 NLT, 168
54:13 NLT, 165
65:17–25 NKJV, 114

65:20 NKJV, 167

James
1:2–4 NLT, 148
2:19 NLT, 150
4:7 KJV, 143
Jeremiah
3:15–17 NLT, 166
30:9 NKJV, 133
Joel
3:15 NCV, 72
John
1:1–2 NKJV, 18, 19
1:3 NKJV, 20
1:10, 20
1:12 NCV, 33, 34
1:14, 20
1:18 NKJV, 24
1:23–25 NCV, 123
1:29, 123
2:6–10 NCV, 95–96
2:11 NCV, 96
3:1–12 NKJV, 56–61
3:3 NKJV, 59
3:6 NKJV, 59
3:7–8 NKJV, 60
3:8 NKJV, 94
3:10 NKJV, 60
3:12 NKJV, 61
3:16 NKJV, 50, 155
3:19–20 NCV, 73
3:35 NKJV, 24
4:24, 18
4:24 NKJV, 54
5:21 NKJV, 53
5:22 NCV, 24, 164–65
5:37 NCV, 84
5:37 NKJV, 119
6:44 NLT, 176
6:45 NLT, 165
6:46 NLT, 84, 119
6:63 NCV, 52

7:24 NKJV, 166
8:56 KJV, 84
10:24–36 NKJV, 43–45
12:32 NLT, 176
12:47–48 NCV, 164
14:2 NKJV, 122
14:12 NCV, 102
14:15 NKJV, 150
14:23 NKJV, 24
16:28 NKJV, 35
17:4 NKJV, 25
17:5 NCV, 23
17:24 NCV, 23
18:36 NKJV, 139
18:36–37 NKJV, 128
1 John
1:1 KJV, 21
2:3–6 NCV, 149
3:1 NCV, 34
3:2 NCV, 35
3:2 NKJV, 55, 77
3:4, 142
3:4 KJV, 77
3:4 NKJV, 77
3:9 NKJV, 77
3:11 NIV, 152
4:12 NKJV, 120
2 John
1:3 NKJV, 22
1:9 NKJV, 22
Jude
1:14–15 KJV, 128

Leviticus
19:18 NKJV, 152
Luke
2:9–14 NKJV, 92
3:38 NKJV, 28
6:31 NCV, 152
6:35 NCV, 152
8:10 NKJV, 13, 177
8:17 NKJV, 15

13:3 NKJV, 153–54
13:5 NKJV, 153–54
13:28 NLT, 133
19:10 KJV, 171
19:11–27 NLT, 137–38
20:36 NLT, 82
22:15–16 NCV, 87
22:18 NCV, 87
22:29–30 NCV, 86
22:30 NCV, 134
22:41–42 NCV, 25
22:41–42 NKJV, 25
24:39 NKJV, 18
24:41–43 NCV, 86

Malachi
4:1–3 KJV, 154
Mark
4:11 NLT, 13, 176–77
16:5–6 NCV, 93
Matthew
2:6 KJV, 126
5:5 NKJV, 108
5:9 KJV, 33
5:19 NCV, 134
5:43–48 NIV, 152
6:10 KJV, 108
7:21–23 NLT, 150
10:14–15 NLT, 169
11:25 NIV, 15
13:11 NKJV, 13–14
13:34–35 NCV, 14
13:41–43 NKJV, 79
13:43 NKJV, 82
16:27 NIV, 147
17:1–2 NCV, 81
18:12–14 NIV, 171
18:21–22 NLT, 173
22:39 NKJV, 152
24:29–31 NKJV, 72
24:31 NCV, 71
28:2–6 NCV, 92–93

Micah
4:1–4 NKJV, 117–18
5:2 KJV, 21
5:2 NKJV, 126

Nahum
1:5 NCV, 116
Numbers
12:8 NKJV, 91

1 Peter
3:18 KJV, 52
4:1–2 NLT, 148
5:1 NLT, 38, 71
5:4 NKJV, 38, 71
2 Peter
1:2–4 KJV, 40
1:2–4 NIV, 40–41
1:2–4 NKJV, 40
1:2–4 NLT, 41
3:9 NLT, 172
Philippians
2:9–11 NKJV, 168
2:15 NIV, 34
3:21 NCV, 54, 77
Proverbs
25:2 NIV, 14
Psalm
9:8 NIV, 128
14:1 NKJV, 140
25:14 NKJV, 15
37:9–11 KJV, 108
37:22 NKJV, 108
44:21 NKJV, 90
67:4 NKJV, 128
73:27 NIV, 50
82:6 NKJV, 42, 45
119:40 KJV, 52
119:156 KJV, 52
136:2 NKJV, 172–73

Revelation

1:14–15 NKJV, 29
1:14–16 NCV, 55, 78
2:7 NKJV, 89, 179
2:10 NCV, 150–51
2:11 NKJV, 179
2:17 NKJV, 179
2:17 NLT, 88
2:26–27 KJV, 130–31
2:26–27 NKJV, 179
3:5 NKJV, 179
3:12 NKJV, 179–80
3:20 NIV, 86
3:21 NKJV, 131, 180
5:9–10 KJV, 131
5:10 NCV, 108
6:14 NKJV, 116
8:2 NLT, 74
8:6 NLT, 74
8:7 NKJV, 74–75
8:8–9 NKJV, 75
10:7 NCV, 75
11:15 NKJV, 76
16:18 NCV, 117
17:14 NCV, 129
19:9 NCV, 88
19:13 NKJV, 21
19:20 NCV, 160
20:4 NLT, 165
20:4–6 NCV, 131
20:4–6 NLT, 156
20:10 NLT, 160
20:12–13 NLT, 158
20:15 NCV, 154
20:15 NLT, 159
21:2–3 NLT, 119
21:7 NKJV, 180
21:8 NIV, 154, 160
21:14 NCV, 134
21:16 KJV, 120
21:16 NCV, 120
21:18–21 NCV, 122
21:21 NKJV, 123

21:22 NCV, 123
21:23 NKJV, 79
22:2 NKJV, 89
Romans
2:7 NKJV, 41
2:13 KJV, 134
3:10 NCV, 163
3:23 NCV, 163
6:12 NKJV, 51
6:15 NLT, 171
6:23 KJV, 154
6:23 NKJV, 51
8:5–8 NLT, 142
8:11 KJV, 51

8:12–18 NLT, 146
8:14 NKJV, 33
8:16 KJV, 33
8:18 NKJV, 38
8:19–23 NLT, 178
8:29 NLT, 38
11:8 NLT, 176
11:25–33 NLT, 174–75
11:33 NKJV, 90
16:25 NKJV, 12
16:25–26 NCV, 32

1 Samuel
2:3 NKJV, 90

1 Thessalonians
4:15–17 NCV, 73
5:21 KJV, 6
1 Timothy
1:15–16 NCV, 172
4:7–8 NKJV, 143
4:7–8 NLT, 143
2 Timothy
2:12 NKJV, 130

Zechariah
2:10–12 NCV, 106
8:3 NIV, 105

8:4–5 NIV, 110
8:16 KJV, 166
14:3–5 NCV, 106–7
14:9–11 NLT, 109
14:16 NKJV, 87
14:16–17 NKJV, 109

Acknowledgments

With the utmost respect and humility, I thank God our Father and our Lord and Savior Jesus Christ for providing the inspiration and strength to complete this message, helping me convey the Good News of glory that's breathtaking and magnificent beyond compare.

I also thank all of the heroes who gave their lives over hundreds of years writing and compiling the Word of God, making sure the Bible survived to this day so the wonderful news can be shared with all humanity.

Special thanks to Bob Barney, editor of ThePlainTruth.com, for encouraging the use of red letters for all of God's personal remarks, especially in the Old Testament.

About the Author

Joe Kovacs is a Bible-believing Christian, unaffiliated with any church or denomination, and author of the Amazon #1 bestseller, *Shocked by the Bible: The Most Astonishing Facts You've Never Been Told.*

He's an award-winning journalist and broadcaster who has run newsrooms in television, radio, and online for more than 25 years, both in the United States and overseas.

A frequent media guest, Kovacs has appeared on *The O'Reilly Factor* on the Fox News Channel as well as countless radio shows across America and the world, including *Coast to Coast AM.*

The book's website is www.thedivinesecret.com.